# Grace in the Middle of Chaos

# Grace in the Middle of Chaos

*Life Be Life'n...But God Still God'n*

**Candace Travis**

Transforming Woman LLC

Chicago, IL

This is a memoir. The events and conversations in this book have been recreated from the author's memory and perspective. Some names and identifying details have been changed to protect the privacy of individuals.

Published by Transforming Woman LLC

Chicago, Illinois

Paperback ISBN: 979-8-9956000-0-8

Hardcover ISBN: 979-8-9956000-1-5

eBook ISBN: 979-8-9956000-2-2

First Edition, 2026

# Contents

# Dedications

**To My Dad — Curtis Travis**

You were my first protector. The first man who showed me what love, loyalty, and showing up really looked like.

You never needed a reason to be there for me. You were just there — proud of me, covering me, loving me through every season, every decision, every version of me. Even when life didn't unfold the way either of us imagined, you never stopped showing up.

You loved my children the same way you loved me — completely. And I'll always be grateful they got to know that kind of grandfather love.

You taught me what presence feels like. What safety feels like. What it means to be loved without having to earn it.

I miss you every single day.

But the way you loved me still lives in me.

And I carry that forward.

**To My Mom — Sylvia**

You were strong. Structured. Tough when you needed to be.

Growing up, we did not always understand each other, but as I got older, I began to see just how much of who I am came from you.

Your strength. Your resilience. The lessons you poured into me that still guide me today.

And somewhere along the way, our relationship grew into something deeper — friendship.

Now we can talk about anything. Laugh about everything. Sometimes I forget you're even my mom because you've become one of my closest friends.

I am who I am because of you.

And I love you for that.

**To Gary**

Life and family are not always simple.

But this is what I can say: you have always been there for this family, especially for the grandchildren who absolutely adore you.

They know that if they call, you will show up. Whether that means a long drive, a phone call, or simply being present when they need you most.

No one is perfect, but showing up still matters.

And I appreciate the ways you have continued to show up for this family.

**To My Big Sister — Kenisha**

We fought like cats and dogs growing up.

But nobody outside of us was ever allowed to mess with either one of us.

You have walked through storms that required a strength most people will never understand. And you are still standing. Still fighting. Still growing.

You call me your little big sister.

But I hope you know something — I admire your resilience more than you realize.

I see you.

And I love you.

Always.

**To My Sister — Purlanda**

My best friend. My silly girl.

The one I never imagined doing life without.

Losing you left a space in my life that will never truly be filled. But the memories we shared, the laughter, the bond we had — those things live with me every single day.

Sometimes I still catch myself wanting to turn and tell you something.

And in those moments, I smile.

Because I know love like ours doesn't disappear.

It just changes form.

I love you forever.

**To My Brother — Jalen**

Ten years apart, but that never mattered.

You've been my baby brother since the day you were born, and somehow over the years you also became one of my closest confidants.

We can talk about anything — life, business, dreams, money, family, everything. We push each other to grow, to win, to build something bigger than ourselves.

You're an amazing uncle to my kids, and I know that no matter what, you're always going to show up for the people you love.

That means more to me than you probably know.

I'm proud to be your big sister.

Always in your corner.

**To My Sisters — Crissy and Courtney**

Curtis's Girls.

Also known as Curtis's 3 C's.

Candace. Crissy. Courtney.

No matter where life has taken us or the seasons that have come and gone, that bond will always be there. We share the same roots, the same name that Dad was proud to give us, and the same connection that will always tie us together.

I'm grateful that we found our way back to each other and that we continue building our relationship as sisters.

I love you both.

**To Conrad**

Blood doesn't always determine who becomes family.

You've been a brother to me in ways that matter far more than labels.

During some of the hardest seasons of my life, you showed up — sitting with me, watching movies, talking through life, or simply being present when I needed someone.

Those moments meant more than you probably realized.

And even now, we can pick up the phone and talk about life like no time has passed.

I'm grateful to have you in my life.

Always.

**To My Children — Laniyah, Ronnie, and Lavell Jr. (Mann)**

You are my greatest chapters — the ones I would write again every time.

Everything I've fought through, healed from, and built has always been for you.

You've seen the real version of me — the struggles, the rebuilding, the growth.

And through it all, you have given my life a purpose deeper than anything else.

Being your mother is the greatest honor I will ever have.

And there is a poem in this book written just for you.

**To Monique — Moe**

If you know me, you know Moe.

More than my cousin — you are my sister, my ride-or-die, my person. We've loved each other, supported each other, and kept each other grounded through so many seasons of life.

We've always had the kind of bond where we could be honest with each other, laugh until we cried, and still be there through the darkest moments too.

And yes — even though that mouth of yours used to get us in trouble while I was trying to get us out of it, I still wouldn't trade you for nothing.

I love you deeply.

You already know the rest.

**To Keneasha E.**

My best friend. My sister by life, not just by title.

You came into my life right on time and somehow became part of me and mine in a way that feels like you were always supposed to be there. My family loves you. My children know you as Auntie. And no matter how much time passes, that love never changes.

We don't have to talk every day to know what it is. We've laughed without words, cried without needing explanations, and carried each other through seasons most people would never fully understand.

You are one of my forever people.

And I love you like family — because to me, you are.

**To My Fab Five**

You know who you are.

Different seasons. Different stories. Same real love.

We may not talk every day, but when it matters, we show up. Birthdays, babies, grief, wins, hard seasons, healing seasons — somehow we always find our way back to each other.

That kind of friendship is rare.

And I never take it for granted.

**To Rob — Puggy**

My favorite homie.

We've been friends since we were kids, and you knew me in ways very few people ever did.

You were there through conversations, laughter, life changes, and everything in between.

You told me that when the pandemic ended we were going out — that I needed a night to breathe again after everything I had been through.

We never got that night.

But what we did have was real friendship — and that is something I will carry with me forever.

You meant more to me than words can fully capture.

**To My Clients and Challengers**

Many of you came into my life looking for transformation.

What you may not realize is that you helped transform me too.

Watching your growth, courage, and determination reminded me that change is always possible.

Your stories poured strength back into mine.

Thank you for trusting me.

**To Everyone Who Picked Up This Book**

You didn't have to choose this story.

But you did.

My hope is that somewhere in these pages you see a piece of yourself — and realize that healing, growth, and grace are possible even in the middle of chaos.

Thank you for being here.

## To My Future Husband

There was a time when I thought I would never open my heart again.

Pain has a way of making you confuse walls with wisdom. But healing has a way of teaching you the difference.

I've done the work. I've faced the hard parts of myself. I've grown into the woman I was always becoming. Not perfect — but whole in the places that matter. Soft where I used to be guarded. Wise where I used to be wounded.

So, wherever you are, I want you to know this: I still believe in love. Real love. Steady love. Safe love. The kind that doesn't need performance, fear, or games to survive.

I'm ready now. Not from desperation. Not from fantasy. But from healing.

And when the time is right, I'll meet you there — fully, honestly, and with the kind of love I was always meant to give.

# INTRODUCTION

Life Be Life'n… But God Still God'n

"Life will knock you down more than once… but as long as you keep getting back up, the story isn't over yet."
— *Coach Candace TW*

Before you go any further —

I need you to know something.

This is not another self-help book.
This is not another motivational speech dressed up in chapters.
This is not another I had a hard life and look at me now story where everything wraps up clean at the end with a bow on it.

This is real.
This is raw.
This is lived.

This is a woman who has been broken in ways she never planned for, rebuilt herself more times than she counted, smiled through storms that would have leveled most people — and is still standing.

Still standing.
Still breathing.
Still becoming.

Not because life got easy.

Because she refused to let it be the last word.

If you are reading this book, chances are life has been life'n for you too.

And when I say life be life'n —
I mean really life'n.

The kind where one minute you think everything is finally coming together — and the next minute something knocks the wind clean out of you.

A divorce. A breakup.
Family problems. Relocation.
Business setbacks. Unexpected debt.
An injury that slows you down.
Losing a job. Getting laid off.
A pandemic nobody saw coming.
A loss that grief grabs hold of and will not let go.
Or a child making choices you never raised them to make.

Yeah.

That kind of life'n.
The kind that changes you whether you're ready or not.

Life has a way of humbling you whether you asked for the lesson or not. Whether you were ready or not. Whether it was fair or not.

And it does not wait for a convenient time.

Let me be honest with you before we even get started.

My life does not look the way I thought it would.

And for a long time, I thought I had to wait until it did before I could tell this story. I thought the ending needed to be perfect. I thought I needed to arrive somewhere clean and put together before I had the right to speak.

But here is what I learned —

the waiting was the lie.

I was not behind.
I was being built.

The story was always happening. Right in the middle of the mess. Right in the middle of the rebuilding. Right in the middle of the not yet and the not sure and the Lord what is going on.

So I stopped waiting to feel ready.
I stopped waiting for perfect.

And I picked up the pen.

Because some stories don't ask for permission.

They just rise.

I have had seasons where I felt like I was on top.

Debt-free.
Running my own gym studio.
Traveling.
Standing on stage as a competitor.
Speaking to rooms full of people.
Feeling strong. Feeling focused.
Feeling like everything was finally lining up.

And then —

life shifted.

More than once.

I have had to start all the way over again. Climb back up. Get my footing. Think I was finally moving forward — and then something else showed up and knocked me back down.

Business changes. Relationship confusion. Family struggles. Financial setbacks. And moments where I looked up and asked the same question a lot of us have asked at some point:

"Did I do something wrong?"

Or is this just life… being life?

Maybe you have asked that too.

Maybe you have had those nights where you are praying, trying to stay positive, trying to stay faithful — but deep down you are still wondering why life feels so heavy. Why every time you get one step up, something pulls you two steps back.

And let us be honest.

We live in a world where everybody looks like they have it all together.

Perfect relationship. Perfect house.
Perfect money. Perfect body.
Perfect family. Perfect everything.

But behind a lot of those pictures is real life.

Stress. Struggles. Bills. Pressure. Fear.

The illusion of having it all together
when privately you are trying to figure out your next move.

I know that feeling.
I know it intimately.

I have lived that feeling.

I have smiled in public while quietly fighting battles no one else could see. I have shown up strong because people expected me to be strong. I have kept moving forward even when my heart was tired and my body was running on faith and fumes.

This book is not about pretending life is perfect.

You see enough of that already.

This book is about what happens when life is not.

It is about learning how to keep your faith when things do not go according to the plan you had in your head. It is about protecting your peace when everything around you feels like chaos. It is about realizing that sometimes the biggest battle you are fighting is not outside of you —

it is inside you.

And if you don't learn how to fight there —
you will keep losing everywhere else.

Your mind. Your fears.
Your past. Your doubts.

The pressure you put on yourself to have everything figured out.

The shame you carry from things that were never your fault.

The chains you are finally ready to break.

I also want to say this — and I am going to be real with you from the jump.

I am not a perfect Christian.

I do not read my Bible every single day. I am not in church every Sunday. I have rarely — but occasionally — said words I should not have said. I have stayed in things I should have left sooner. And I have made choices that did not exactly line up with what I was taught.

I am not going to sit here and pretend otherwise.

And I am definitely not here to thump you over the head with a Bible and tell you that you are doing it wrong.

But here is what I know for certain —

I love God deeply.
Not perfectly. But honestly.

And that love has carried me through everything you are about to read.

So, you do not have to share my exact beliefs or my background or my journey to receive what is in these pages. You do not have to be a Christian. You do not have to have it all figured out spiritually.

I walk by faith. I believe in the power of your words. I believe that healing — mentally, emotionally, physically, spiritually — is available to anyone willing to do the work.

That is my foundation.

But this book is not here to tell you that yours has to look like mine.

It is here for anyone who has ever been knocked down and had to find a reason to get back up. Anyone who has ever survived something they did not think they would survive. Anyone who has ever looked in the mirror on a hard morning and wondered if the person staring back still had something worth building.

This is for you.

No matter your age. No matter your background. No matter where you are or how far you feel from where you thought you would be.

Through all of it —
the rebuilding, the praying, the crying, the pressing forward —
one truth has never changed.

Life be life'n…
but God will forever and always be God'n.

Even when I do not understand the timing.
Even when I am rebuilding again.
Even when I am tired.

There is one scripture I keep coming back to. Whenever life is really life'n and I am sitting there asking what is going on — this is the one:

2 Corinthians 4:8–9 —
"We are hard pressed on every side, but not crushed; perplexed, but not in despair; persecuted, but not abandoned; struck down, but not destroyed."

That scripture is saying:

You may feel pressure —
but you are not finished.

You may feel confused —
but you are not without direction.

You may feel attacked —
but you have not been abandoned.

You may get knocked down —
but you are not destroyed.

You are still here.

And as long as you are still here —

there is still purpose attached to your life.

There is still something in you that has not been finished yet.

If life has been pressing you, confusing you, stretching you, forcing you to start over —

This book is for you.

Not because I have all the answers.

But because I have lived the questions.

And I kept going anyway.

This is not about having everything figured out.

This is about learning how to keep moving when you don't.

About finding grace in the places you least expect it.

About realizing that even in the middle of chaos —

you are still being carried.

About rising from the ashes of everything that tried to finish you —

not unburned,
but undefeated.

Not untouched,
but unbroken.

Life may be life'n.

But you are still standing.

And that means the story is not over yet.

Let's start at the beginning.

"The comeback is always louder than the setback — if you don't quit on yourself."
— *Coach Candace TW*

## CHAPTER 1

# When Life Don't Go According to Plan

"Stop apologizing for where you are. You're not behind — you're being redirected. Trust the detour."

— *Coach Candace TW*

Let me ask you something.

What did you think your life would look like by now?

At some point, we all had a picture in our head.

How things would go.

How things would feel.

How everything would come together.

And life?

Life has a way of happening in between those plans.

And it does not ask your permission first.

And when I say life happened —

I don't mean a little bit.

I mean the kind that comes in and rearranges everything you thought you had figured out.

Your finances.

Your family.

Your relationships.

Your business.

Your body.

Your peace.

Sometimes all at once.

And you're standing there like…

Wait.

This wasn't the plan.

Starting over is a different kind of pain.

It's not always loud.

Sometimes it's quiet.

Sometimes it looks like sitting in your car a little longer before you go in the house.

Sometimes it looks like staring at the ceiling at 4 a.m. thinking,

How in the world am I back here again?

Sometimes it looks like smiling in public, encouraging everybody else, posting something positive —

and then going home thinking,

Lord… I thought I was past this part.

That's the part people don't talk about enough.

Everybody loves a comeback story when it's finished.

Everybody claps when they see the glow-up.

The new house.

The business doing well.

The healed version of you.

The "look what God did" moment.

But don't nobody really talk about the middle.

The middle is where your faith gets tested.

The middle is where your confidence gets tested.

The middle is where you start asking yourself questions you thought you already answered.

Did I miss something?

Did I make the wrong turn?

Did I do something wrong?

Why does it feel like every time I get momentum…

something comes and tries to knock the wind out of me.

Meanwhile, social media is doing what it does.

Highlight reels.

Soft life clips.

Matching pajamas.

Trips.

New keys.

"God did it!" captions.

And everybody looks like they got life in a chokehold.

And here you are trying to figure out why your life keeps hitting the remix button.

That'll have you questioning yourself if you let it.

Here's what nobody tells you about plans:

God has a way of editing them.

Not to punish you.

Not because you did something wrong.

But because sometimes the plan you made for yourself

is smaller than the one He has for you.

And the only way to get to the bigger thing…

is to let go of the smaller one.

Even when the letting go feels like losing.

"Everything will happen the way it has to happen… All is well."

I had to learn that starting over does not automatically mean I failed.

Sometimes starting over means life exposed what wasn't stable.

Sometimes starting over means God is shifting you out of something that no longer fits.

Sometimes starting over means you outgrew a version of yourself…

a place…

a relationship…

a mindset…

a plan.

And sometimes starting over means you are being asked to build again —

but this time with more wisdom,

more discernment,

more boundaries,

and a stronger backbone.

That sounds good now.

But when you're in it?

It does not always feel deep and spiritual.

Sometimes it just feels irritating.

Sometimes it feels like,

Lord, I'm tired.

Sometimes it feels like,

Can one thing just work all the way through?

Sometimes it feels like,

I know I'm strong… but I'm a little over these character-building exercises.

And yes — I laugh.

Because if I don't laugh sometimes,

I'll be sitting there looking at the wall like…

Wow.

So, we doing this again?

But here's what I also know:

A setback is not a definition.

A detour is not an identity.

A hard season is not proof that God forgot about you.

And needing to rebuild

does not erase everything you already survived,

built,

learned,

and became.

Nothing is wasted.

Not the years you spent learning.

Not the mistakes you made.

Not the relationships that taught you what you need —

and what you don't.

Not the seasons that stretched you.

Not the heartbreak.

Not the delays.

Not even the disappointment.

It all taught you something.

And some of the strongest parts of you

were built in seasons

you would not have chosen.

So, if you picked up this book in a rebuilding season —

hear me clearly:

You are not weak because you're tired.

You are not behind because life shifted.

You are not a failure because something ended.

And you are not disqualified because you have to begin again.

Sometimes beginning again

is exactly how God reintroduces you to yourself.

Not the version of you that only knew how to function

when everything made sense —

but the version of you that knows how to stand in faith,

move with wisdom,

protect your peace,

and keep going

without needing every detail mapped out first.

That version of you?

Yeah…

She's dangerous in the best way.

Psalm 37:23–24

"The Lord makes firm the steps of the one who delights in him; though he may stumble, he will not fall, for the Lord upholds him with his hand."

What this means to me:

God is not surprised by your stumble.

He already accounted for it.

The stumble doesn't cancel the steps

He ordered for you.

You're not behind.

You're not forgotten.

You're in the middle.

And the middle means…

you're still in the story.

"Be encouraged…

this is just a chapter in your book —

not the whole story."

"The middle of the story is where faith is built. If everything came easy, you wouldn't need it."

— *Coach Candace TW*

## CHAPTER 2

# The Climb, The Fall, and The Climb Again

"Falling down doesn't make you a failure. Staying down does. Get up one more time than life knocks you down — that's the whole game."

— *Coach Candace TW*

Have you ever had a season where everything was working?

Not perfect — but moving.

Growing.

Building.

You could feel the momentum.

And you just knew something good was happening.

I have had that feeling.

And I have lost it more than once.

That is the part nobody puts on their vision board.

Nobody makes a cute graphic that says:

coming soon — the fall.

Nobody posts about starting over —
at least not until they are on the other side of it
and it makes a good testimony.

But in the middle of it?
When you are actually living it?

It is not cute.
It is not inspiring.
It is just hard.

One thing about starting over —
especially when you are grown grown —
is this: It can mess with your identity if you let it.
Because after a while, if you are not grounded,
you start measuring yourself
by what stayed and what did not.

If the business did not make it, what does that say about me?
If I have to start over again, what does that say about me?

If my life does not look the way I imagined by now, what does that say about me?

That is where a lot of people get stuck.

Not in the setback itself —

but in the meaning they attach to it.

I had to learn this the hard way:

A setback is not a definition.

A detour is not an identity.

And needing to rebuild

does not erase everything you already survived,

built, learned, and became.

I had my own gym in Chicago.

My own space. My own clients. My own vision.

And it was working.

I was building something real — and I knew it.

But then the neighborhood started changing.

It got dangerous.

And me and my husband made the decision together — it was time to go. Not because we wanted to. But when you have kids, some decisions are not really decisions. They are just what you do.

So we left.

I told my clients I was moving.

They said they would follow me.

And some of them meant it — for a little while.

But distance is real. Life is real.

And slowly, one by one, they faded.

That is a specific kind of loss.

When something you built does not crash —

it just quietly disappears.

No big dramatic moment.

Just a slow fade.

And you are standing there like —

Okay. Now what.

Then me and my husband separated.

And I had to leave that chapter behind too.

I moved to my mom's house.

Did not have a clear next move.

Did not have a full plan.

And if I am being real —

that was one of those moments

where it could have broke me if I let it.

Because starting over once?

Okay.

But starting over again

after you already thought you rebuilt?

That hits different.

And then the pandemic hit.

Which sounds like the worst possible timing.

But sometimes your biggest pivot

comes disguised as your worst moment.

I got on Zoom.

Started doing online challenges.

Started training people in their living rooms

while I was in mine.

And it took off.

People needed to move.

They needed structure.

They needed somebody to push them.

And I was right there.

That season reminded me of everything Transforming Woman was always meant to be — the name, the mission, the slogan that came straight from scripture: be transformed by the renewing of your mind. Because that is what was happening. Not just for my clients. For me. My mind was shifting. My identity was being rebuilt from the inside out. And the business followed.

Business got good.

Good enough for me to get my own place again.

Good enough to start rebuilding my life on my own terms.

Then the world opened back up.

People went back to work.

Gyms reopened.

Schedules changed.

And just like that — things slowed down again.

I am a single mom.

So, I did what I had to do.

I got a job.

Still coaching. Still building. Still showing up.

But making sure my kids had what they needed.

And then I got injured.

A work injury that forced me to stop.

To sit down.

To step back from everything.

I am not going to dress that season up.

I was stressed.

I was praying.

And I was sitting there like —

God, I have been asking you to get me back to doing what I love — but this is not exactly what I had in mind.

And then I had to laugh.

Because okay, God. I hear you.

Sometimes comfort becomes a cage without you realizing it. I probably would have stayed at that job because it felt safe. And when you are responsible for people, safe can feel like the right decision.

But God had other plans.

And in that forced slowdown — I went all in.

Challenges. Training. Pouring into people.

My posing coach did not hesitate.

Come back. Train here.

No pressure. No judgment.

Just — let's work.

That kind of grace? You do not forget that.

And slowly — things started moving again.

Eventually I got my own gym space again.

And I loved it.

Even with the imperfections.

It felt like everything was finally coming back around.

Classes. Clients. Community.

The vision was alive again.

But things are not always what they look like on the surface.

The place started falling apart.

The landlord was not doing his part.

The furnace went out in the middle of winter.

By the time summer came, there was no air either — same system, same neglect, same landlord who was not fixing anything.

Conditions got bad.

The kind of bad where you cannot in good conscience

keep bringing people into that space.

And then — he wanted to raise the rent.

I tried to make it work.

I always try to make it work.

But there comes a point

where you have to stop holding on

to something that is not holding you.

So I walked away.

Again.

And just like before — my posing coach did not skip a beat.

Come back. Train here. Something better is coming.

Three rebuilds.

Three times I built something and had to let it go.

Three times I had to look at my life and say —

Alright. We doing this again.

I will not tell you it gets easier.

It does not.

If anything, it gets heavier.

Because now you know what it costs.

You know the sacrifice.

You know the time.

You know the energy.

But you also know something else.

There was a season — and if you know the story of Job, you know what I mean — where everything gets stripped. Not just one thing. Everything. And you are standing in the middle of what used to be your life asking God what is going on.

That was real for me.

A season where the business was gone, the marriage was over, the body was healing, and the stability I had worked so hard to build was not there anymore.

And I still showed up.

Not perfectly.

Not without tears.

Not without sitting down and saying —

okay, let me gather myself.

But I showed up.

Because the blueprint is believing in yourself

even when the building has fallen down.

The cheat code is discipline and consistency

when nothing around you is consistent.

And the truth nobody wants to say out loud —

nobody is coming to save you.

Not on your timeline.

Not in the form you imagined.

You have to build toward what is coming.

And what is coming is better.

But you have to keep moving toward it.

Every lesson counts.

Every prayer counts.

Every time you got back up counts.

Every season you survived counts.

Nothing is wasted.

Not the years spent learning.

Not the mistakes made.

Not the relationships that taught you what you need and what you do not.

Not the financial lessons.

Not the heartbreak.

Not the delays.

Not even the disappointment.

It all taught you something.

And strength — real strength —
does not come from what you can do
when everything is going right.

It comes from overcoming
what you thought you could not survive
when everything went wrong.

Some of the strongest parts of you
were built in seasons you would not have chosen.

At some point you stop asking
why is this happening to me —
and you start realizing:

Life be life'n.
But God still God'n.

And every time I thought I was done —

I was not.

Every door that closed

had another one waiting somewhere down the hall.

Not always right away.

Not always where I expected.

But it showed up.

She is wiser now. Sharper.

Not because the road was kind —

but because she refused to stay down.

She built something from what was left every single time. And what she is building now has roots that nothing can shake, because they were grown in seasons that tried to take everything.

That is grace in the middle of chaos.

And it will show up for you too.

Jeremiah 29:11 — "For I know the plans I have for you, declares the Lord, plans to prosper you and not to harm you, plans to give you hope and a future."

What this means to me: God already wrote the next chapter before this one fell apart. The setback did not catch Him off guard. He already planned what comes next. Your job is just to get back up and keep walking toward it.

"Every time I fell, I thought that was the end. But every time I got back up, I realized it was just the beginning of something better." — *Coach Candace TW*

## CHAPTER 3

# Energy Vampires and Empty Cups

"Life be life'n… but God still God'n. And that's exactly why I had to stop letting everybody sip from my peace like it was free refills."

— *Coach Candace TW*

Let me say something that might not feel good at first.

Everybody does not deserve access to you.

Not your time.

Not your energy.

Not your peace.

Not your presence.

And if you do not learn that the right way —

life will teach you the hard way.

There was a time in my life where I felt like I had to be everything for everybody.

The strong one.

The dependable one.

The one people could call.

The one people could lean on.

And do not get me wrong — that is a beautiful thing.

Until it starts draining you.

Because what I had to learn is this:

You can be pouring into everybody else

and still be running on empty yourself.

That is a dangerous place to live.

From the outside, it looks like you are strong.

But on the inside, you are exhausted.

Mentally. Emotionally. Spiritually.

Soul-tired. Mind-tired. Emotionally stretched-thin tired.

The kind of tired where you can still smile, still answer the phone, still show up, still teach the class, still tell somebody else you got this — and then go home, close the door, and cry because life is life'n and you are trying to figure things out yourself.

That kind of tired.

And the wild part? Some of the same people you are pouring into do not even realize they are draining you.

And let me say this too — because it matters:

Not everybody who drains you is doing it on purpose.

Some people are not vampires.

Some people are just thirsty.

They are used to you being the source. The well they come to when they need something. The person who always has something to give. And because you have always given — they keep coming back.

Not out of malice.

Out of habit.

Out of need.

Out of not knowing any better.

That does not make it okay. But it does make it human.

And understanding the difference between someone who is intentionally taking from you and someone who is simply used to you giving — that is where wisdom lives.

Because your response to both might look similar from the outside. A boundary is a boundary. But on the inside, one comes from self-protection and one comes from grace.

You can have both.

You can protect your cup and still love the people who were drinking from it.

You just have to stop letting them drink until there is nothing left.

Not everybody in your life is a vampire. Some people are just thirsty.

But either way —

you still have to protect your cup.

And if you never set boundaries — they will keep taking because you keep giving.

At some point, I had to get real with myself.

Not with them — with me.

Because the truth is, people will treat you how you allow them to.

And access? Access is taught.

That is when I started moving different. Not funny. Not bitter. Not distant.

Just intentional.

And here is something I had to correct in myself — because I have heard it said a thousand times and it sounds comforting:

God won't put more on you than you can bear.

That is not a scripture.

God does not hand you five jobs, three toxic relationships, a business, and somebody else's emotional baggage and say you can handle it. A lot of what we are carrying, we chose. Or we allowed. Or we did not know how to say no to.

The truth is: life will absolutely feel like too much sometimes. You will have seasons where you feel overwhelmed, stretched, and like you cannot carry it.

But God will give you the strength to endure what you thought would break you.

That is the difference. You are not carrying it alone — even when it feels that way.

And when you understand that, you stop trying to be everything for everybody. You stop overextending yourself. You stop answering every call. You stop explaining every boundary.

And you start choosing peace.

"Life be life'n, but God still God'n — and one of the ways He protects me is by teaching me when to pull back, be still, and stop handing my peace to people who never knew how to handle it."

— *Coach Candace TW*

My phone stays on Do Not Disturb for a reason.

Not because I am ignoring people.

Not because I do not care.

Because I am protecting my peace. There is a difference.

The people who truly need access to me have it. My children. My mom. A very small, intentional circle of people who will not abuse it — the ones where if they are calling, it matters.

That is it.

Everybody else can wait.

And that might sound harsh to some people. But what is really harsh is constantly abandoning yourself to be available to everybody else.

I am not everybody's emergency contact.

Say that again.

I am not everybody's emergency contact.

Because some of us have been walking around like unpaid emotional paramedics — rushing to every fire, every crisis, every breakdown, every draining conversation — and then wondering why we feel empty.

Your cup has been on E.

As a coach, I put some of my clients through detoxes.

And what I have learned from watching them go through that process is that it is never just physical.

When you commit to cleaning out what no longer serves your body — the processed stuff, the excess, everything causing inflammation — your body starts releasing what it has been holding. And it is not always comfortable at first. Some people get headaches. Some people feel more tired before they feel better. Some people break out.

Because what is coming out needed to come out.

Your body was holding it. Storing it. Carrying it.

And when you finally give it permission to release — it does.

Your life works the same way.

When you start being intentional about what you allow in — the conversations, the energy, the people, the environments — things start shifting. Old habits surface. Old mindsets come up. Old relationships that made sense in a previous season start to feel heavy in a new one.

If you are not careful, you will think something is wrong because everything feels uncomfortable.

Nothing is wrong.

You are detoxing.

And some things — some people, some spaces, some habits — were never meant to stay once you started healing.

That is not a punishment. That is a process.

I noticed this shift in my own life gradually.

There were people I used to talk to constantly — and over time, the conversations just started to feel different. Not bad. Just different. The season had changed. We had grown in different directions.

And that is okay.

Sometimes it is just growth happening in different directions at the same time.

If you are not careful, you will try to hold on to people the same way even when the season has changed.

Everything does not go with you into your next level.

And that does not make it bad. It does not mean the love is gone. It just means you are honest enough to let things shift naturally instead of forcing what is no longer fitting.

I still love those people. That has not changed. But love does not always require the same level of access it once did. And real love — the kind that is rooted in something genuine — can survive the shift.

There are people who will sit in your presence and pull from you without ever pouring back.

Energy vampires.

Not always loud. Not always obvious. Sometimes they smile. Sometimes they laugh with you. Sometimes they say they love you.

But every time you leave them, you feel tired. And you do not even know why.

I had to start paying attention to that.

Not judging people — but paying attention.

Because your energy is currency. And you do not get to spend it everywhere.

Everybody who wants access to me is not automatically safe for me.

Say it again.

Everybody who wants access to me is not automatically safe for me.

Some folks want to be your friend but really want your information. Some want to date you but really want your light. Some want to do business with you but really want you to carry the vision while they come along for the ride. They like what you carry. They like what happens around you. They like what being connected to you does for them.

But liking your light and knowing how to honor you are two very different things.

That is where discernment matters.

Not everybody is meant to go where you are going.

That used to frustrate me. Because I am the kind of person who wants everybody to win. If I learn something helpful, I want to share it. I am not a gatekeeper — that has never been me.

But I had to realize: everybody does not have the same vision. Everybody does not want the same life. Everybody does not want growth, risk, or even healing.

And that is okay.

I can love people without needing them to understand every part of my path.

Say it.

I can love people without needing them to understand every part of my path.

Some people are assignments. Some people are lessons. And some people are just not meant to have access to you anymore.

And that does not make you cold. That makes you clear.

This chapter is not about cutting everybody off.

It is about wisdom.

Knowing when to answer and when not to. Knowing when to pour and when to pull back. Knowing when somebody loves you and when somebody loves what you do for them. Knowing when a season has shifted. Knowing when your peace is costing you too much to keep negotiating.

You are allowed to evolve.

You are allowed to need more quiet. More peace. You are allowed to share less. To go inward for a season. To stop overexplaining. To let some connections shift naturally. To love people from a distance. To choose peace over proving you are a good person.

And if somebody does not understand that? That is okay. Not every chapter of your growth requires an audience. Some chapters they just have to witness from afar.

Repeat this to yourself:

My peace is not rude. It is necessary.

My boundaries are not rejection. They are protection.

Everybody cannot carry my heart, my vision, or my energy.

I can be loving and still say no.

I can pour into others without abandoning myself.

I do not have to be available to be valuable.

I do not have to drain myself to prove I care.

Life be life'n… but God still God'n — and I do not have to panic when I choose peace.

Your assignment:

Take a moment and really check your life. Not surface level. Be honest.

Who drains you? What environments leave you feeling heavy? What conversations feel forced? Where are you overextending yourself just to keep the peace?

Now ask yourself this:

What would change if I protected my energy the way I protect everything else?

Then do something about it. Not tomorrow. Now.

Because the life you are asking God for requires a version of you that knows how to protect it.

Matthew 11:28 — "Come to me, all you who are weary and burdened, and I will give you rest."

What this means to me: Even God knew we were not meant to carry everything alone. He did not say figure it out. He did not say push through. He said come to me — and I will give you rest. That is not just for Sunday mornings. That is an open invitation for every moment you feel like you are drowning in everyone else's needs. You are allowed to put it down.

"Everybody can't go where you're going. Some people are assignments. Some people are lessons. And some people are just not meant to have access to you anymore."

— *Coach Candace TW*

# CHAPTER 4

## Shame Ain't Yours to Carry

"The things that happened to you were never a reflection of your worth. You didn't ask for it then, and you don't have to carry it now."

— *Coach Candace TW*

Shame is heavy.

That is the first thing I want to say.

Not the loud, dramatic kind of heavy where you are visibly falling apart. The quiet kind. The kind that makes you function perfectly on the outside while something inside you has been whispering lies for so long that you stopped noticing it was not your own voice anymore.

Because that is what shame does when it gets comfortable.

It gets into your choices. Your relationships. Your body. Your voice. How you see yourself. What you tolerate. What you think you have to accept. What you believe you deserve.

This is what I didn't understand back then:

A lot of us are carrying shame that was never ours to begin with.

Read that again. Sit with it.

Because that was me. For a long time, that was me.

I was a happy child.

Full of life. Vivid imagination. Planned my whole future out before I even got to high school — school, career, love, a family, all of it. I was going to do everything right. I knew exactly who I was going to be.

And then things happened to me that I did not have words for.

The first time, I was young. The person who hurt me was older, but still young themselves. What happened between us had a name I did not know yet — some people call it playing house. It felt wrong. It felt yucky. It made me uncomfortable in my own skin in a way I could not explain. But I also did not fully understand what it was, and neither did they — because somewhere in their own story, something similar had happened to them. Cycles like that do not always come from malice.

Sometimes they come from wounds that were never treated, passed down before anyone knew to stop them.

That does not make it okay. But it does help explain it.

The second time was different. The person was older. Trusted. Someone with access to me because the adults around me believed they were safe. What happened was not playing. It was a violation. And when I did not say anything — when I swallowed it and kept moving — they found a way to make it my fault. Because I had started growing into my body. Because my hips came in and I stopped hiding them.

That was the explanation I was given.

And I was young enough, and broken enough, to believe it.

And somewhere in all of that…

I started wondering if something was wrong with me.

Like… why does this keep happening to me?

Let me be clear: fitted jeans are not an invitation. Hips that God gave you are not an invitation. A girl discovering she likes how she looks is not asking for anything from anyone. What happened to me was not caused by what I wore. It was caused by someone who made a choice they had no right to make.

But I did not know how to hold that truth then. So instead, I held the shame.

I had always written. Since I was young — maybe fifth or sixth grade — I kept journals and wrote poems about my life. Happy ones at first. Funny ones. Little observations about my days and my world.

But after things started happening to me, the poems changed.

I started writing about feeling like I was sealed inside a jar. Like someone was slowly pouring sand over me and screwing the lid down tight. Like I was drowning in something thick and slow, and everyone around me was going about their lives not noticing.

Those journals were the only place I told the truth.

And then one day, someone found them.

Someone I had trusted read my private words without my permission — and instead of seeing the pain of a girl trying to survive, they made it something dirty. They used my words against me. They turned my attempt to heal into something shameful.

And I felt violated all over again.

After that, I stopped writing.

For a long time, I put the pen down. The one place I had given myself permission to be honest did not feel safe anymore.

There is a woman I want to speak to directly — someone who will know exactly who she is when she reads this.

She loved me. She was warm and funny and her home felt like family. I spent time around her, grew up knowing her, and somewhere in my young heart I had imagined that one day her son and I would end up together.

Then I got pregnant as a teenager.

And when she found out, she said something she almost certainly did not mean the way I heard it. She said she had thought I was going to be her daughter-in-law one day.

She did not call me dirty. She did not say I was ruined.

But I was a hurt girl already drowning in shame, already convinced that what had been done to me had left something on me that other people could see. And what I heard was confirmation of every lie I had already been telling myself.

He won't want you now. You were supposed to be something. And look at you.

I stopped going around that family.

Not because of anything they did intentionally. But because the shame I was already wearing made ordinary moments feel like verdicts.

It would be years — years of growing up, getting married, having children — before I would really be around them again. And even then, something in me still carried the weight of that younger version of myself who had walked away from people she loved because she did not believe she deserved to stay.

That pregnancy — my son, who I love completely — came from a season of quiet destruction.

Once I believed I was dirty, once I accepted that narrative about myself, the choices that followed were not really choices in the way choices are supposed to be. They were dominoes. One falling into the next. A girl who had stopped believing she deserved protection, so she stopped protecting herself.

I am not going to tell the full story of that night. What matters is this: I was a teenager who had been made to feel worthless by things that were done to her, and I made a decision from that broken place. Not because someone forced me. But because I had already decided, somewhere beneath the surface, that it did not matter. That I did not matter.

And then I was pregnant.

And the shame multiplied.

Teen mom. Another check against you. Another thing to carry. See? This is just who you are.

That is how shame compounds. It does not stay in one place. It spreads into every open wound and tells you that all of it —

every hard thing, every painful outcome, every broken season — is simply what you deserve.

And some people never get out from under that.

I know this because I have worked with them.

Over the years of coaching and pouring into people, I have sat with women who gained weight on purpose — not because of what they ate, but because of what happened to them. They made their bodies bigger believing it would keep people from wanting them the way they had been wanted before, in ways that hurt them. They carried weight as armor. As a wall.

Shame shows up in the body. In the choices. In the silence people keep for decades.

Some people never put it down.

Some people took their lives because of it.

And that is exactly why I am writing this chapter. Not to center my pain, but to say: if any part of this story sounds familiar — if you have been carrying something you were never supposed to carry — I need you to hear this clearly:

What happened to you is not the same thing as who you are.

Say that to yourself.

What happened to me is not the same thing as who I am.

Again.

What happened to me is not the same thing as who I am.

Healing from shame is not a single moment. It is a process. And for me, part of that process was therapy — finally sitting in a room with someone who did not know the people involved, which meant I did not have to protect anyone. I could just tell the truth. And the truth, when you finally speak it out loud to someone who receives it without judgment, starts to lose some of its power over you.

My therapist helped me understand that many of my choices — the ones I had judged myself harshest for — were not random. They were connected. They traced back to a little girl who had been taught by experience that her body was not her own, that her voice did not matter, that she was lucky if anyone wanted her at all.

Once I could see that, I could start to separate what happened to me from who I was.

And I could start to forgive.

I want to speak directly to the people whose actions are woven into this story — because I know some of them will read these pages.

To the one who was young: I forgive you. Fully. What you did was wrong and it affected me deeply. But I understand that you were also carrying something you had not been taught how to hold. When you came to me with your remorse — I saw someone who had been hurting too. I want you to forgive yourself. I have let it go. You can too.

To the one who was older: I forgive you too. There was no answer you could have given me that would have made it make sense, because there is not one. But I got to say what I needed to say. I got to tell you the truth about the damage. And then I chose to release it — not because it was small, but because I refused to carry it for the rest of my life.

And then there is my mom.

When she found out — even the pieces she found out — something in her shut down.

She was hurt. She was upset. She was a mother who did not know this had been happening to her child, and that realization came with its own kind of pain. But somewhere in the weight of what she was feeling, her embarrassment took up more room than my need did. The shame of not knowing. The shame of not protecting me. What it meant about her. What people might think. It all came flooding in — and instead of setting it aside to show up for me, she went inward with it.

She did not mean to leave me standing there alone in it.

But she did.

And I carried the weight of that for a long time. Not just what happened to me — but the silence that followed. The feeling that even the person who was supposed to be my safe place could not hold what I was carrying.

I want to be clear, so nobody misreads this: my mother was not okay with what happened. She was not indifferent. She was not unbothered. She was a woman who loved me deeply and did not know how to process what she had learned in a way that put me first.

That is a human failure. Not a character one.

And I have lived long enough and healed enough to understand the difference.

Mom — I forgive you. Fully. Not because what I needed in that moment did not matter. It did. But because I understand now that you were standing in your own pain trying to figure out how to hold mine — and you did not have the tools yet.

You gave me your blessing to tell this story. You said: it is yours to tell.

That meant everything.

So, I tell it — not to wound you, but to free us both.

It is time to put it down.

I put mine down. You can put yours down too.

What matters is who we are to each other now. And we built something real.

Forgiveness is not the same as saying it was okay.

It is not pretending it did not happen. It is not erasing the damage. It is not handing back access automatically. It is not weakness.

Forgiveness is deciding that you will not spend the rest of your life being defined by what someone else did to you in a moment when you had no power. It is taking that power back. It is choosing that the story does not end there.

And healing — real healing — does not make you perfect. It makes you aware.

Aware of your patterns. Aware of where old pain has been making new decisions. Aware of what you have been tolerating that you no longer have to. Aware of the lies that got comfortable enough to start sounding like your own voice.

Once you see those things, you cannot unsee them. And that is not a burden — that is freedom.

Before you leave this chapter, I want you to sit with something.

Not a long assignment. Just one honest moment.

Write down one lie that pain taught you about yourself.

Then write the truth beneath it.

Because of what happened to me, I believed I was damaged and unworthy.

Truth: I was wounded. But I was never unworthy. Those are not the same thing.

No rushing. No performing. Just the truth.

Because healing gets louder the moment shame stops running the room.

Psalm 34:18 — "The Lord is close to the brokenhearted and saves those who are crushed in spirit."

What this means to me: He was not far away in those moments. He was closer than the shame, closer than the silence, closer than the lies I had accepted about myself. He saw that little girl. He sees you. And He did not create you to stay crushed. He created you to be restored.

"The moment I stopped wearing shame like it belonged to me was the moment I gave God room to show me who I really was underneath all that pain." — *Coach Candace TW*

After years of silence, I picked the pen back up again. The poems started coming faster than I expected. Some of them are about healing, some about strength, some about grace. It wasn't easy choosing which ones belonged in this book… but these are the ones that helped me find my voice again.

# They Thought Silence Was the End

They found my pages.
Not gently, not like something sacred.
They read my wounds out loud — like they were punchlines.
Laughed at places I was still bleeding from.
Took the only place I knew how to breathe
and turned it into something I had to be ashamed of.
So, I closed the book.
Not just the pages — me.
Folded my voice up small, real small,
tucked her away like something dangerous
nobody was supposed to see.
And the world never knew
what went quiet that day.

But here's what they miscalculated —
You can't silence what God put in somebody on purpose.
You can slow it down. You can bury it.
Yeah.
You can convince a girl for twenty years
that her voice is too much, too loud, too real, too dangerous.
But dangerous to who?
To the lie that said she was nothing?
To the shame that told her to stay small?
To the fear that needed her quiet just to survive?
Yeah.
Dangerous to all.

So when I finally picked the pen back up —
Oh, it wasn't soft. It wasn't polite.
It didn't come back asking, "Is this okay?"
No.
It came back like something

that had been held underwater too long
and finally broke the surface.
Gasping. Shaking. Alive.
And done being silent.

I don't hide my pages anymore.
I don't whisper my truth into journals nobody's supposed to find.
No. I write it. And I hand it to you.
Not because I'm no longer afraid,
but because I finally understood something
they never wanted me to know:
My voice was never the problem.
It was always the answer.

This is for every woman who learned how to shrink just to survive.
For every throat that swallowed words that deserved to be heard.
For every journal hidden under mattresses,
or tucked inside a chest that carried too much in silence.
I see you.
And I need you to hear me clearly —
You don't have to hide anymore.
Your story is not shameful.
Your voice is not dangerous.
It is necessary.

And the silence?
Is silent no more.

## CHAPTER 5

# Who You Love and How You Love

"Sometimes the problem isn't that you loved the wrong people. The problem is that you loved the right people before you fully loved yourself."

— *Coach Candace TW*

One thing about me — when I love, I love hard.

Not halfway.

Not cautiously.

Not with one foot in and one foot out.

If I care about you, you know it. I show up. I encourage you, pray for you, celebrate you, pour into you the way I pour into the people I coach.

That is just who I am. It always has been.

But what nobody tells you when you are growing up is this:

Loving hard can become dangerous when you do not know your own worth yet.

Because when you love deeply but have not fully healed — when you are still carrying things you have not named yet — you sometimes give people access to parts of you they have not earned. And you do it genuinely. Willingly. Believing that if you just love them enough, show up enough, stay long enough, something will shift.

That was me for a long time.

Let me put it to you this way.

If you have ever tried to make gumbo — or looked up a recipe and found fifty different versions of the same dish — you already know.

There are a hundred different ways to do it. Different ingredients. Different steps. Some people follow recipes precisely. Some people cook by feel — a little of this, pull back on that, let it simmer until it becomes something you cannot quite explain but you know when it is right.

That is how I used to love.

I would throw in patience. Pour in forgiveness. Add more understanding. Stir in loyalty. Keep adjusting, keep giving, keep hoping that eventually the pot would turn into something good.

What I had to learn — and this took time — is that if the base is not right, if the foundation is off, it does not matter what you add later. It is not going to come together the way it should.

You cannot season your way out of the wrong relationship. You cannot out-love someone's unwillingness to grow. You cannot pour yourself into something until it becomes what it was never meant to be.

That is not a failure of love.

That is just the truth about love.

The hardest question I ever had to sit with was not why did this end.

It was: why did I stay so long?

And the honest answer had layers.

Part of it was my heart — I genuinely loved. Part of it was my belief in commitment, in family, in not walking away. Part of it was my children and wanting them to grow up in a whole home.

But underneath all of that was something therapy helped me finally name: I had learned early in life to work for approval. To earn my place. To show people I was good enough, loyal enough, worthy enough. And when you carry that into how you love, you stop choosing from wholeness and start choosing from need.

You love like you are still trying to prove something.

When you see that pattern clearly, you cannot unsee it.

My marriage taught me more about myself than almost anything else in my life. Not because it was all bad — it was not. We grew up together in many ways. We built a family. We had seasons of real love.

And the fact that we found our way to a real friendship — that we can be in the same room, at the same table, and choose peace — I want to be clear about something.

That did not happen by accident.

And it definitely did not happen overnight.

It was built slowly. Through individual healing on both sides. Through choosing again and again not to let bitterness write the ending of something that still had purpose — because we share children, and they were always watching.

I prayed for him. Genuinely. Not performatively. I prayed that he would heal. That he would grow into the father he was meant to be. And slowly, those prayers started being answered.

People do not always understand that. They want you to be angry. They want the war. They expect bitterness as proof that you were hurt.

But bitterness would have cost me more than it ever would have cost him.

Holding onto resentment, carrying that weight in your body — that is not strength. That is stress. And stress is not just emotional. It shows up physically. It elevates cortisol. It disrupts sleep, weight, immunity, healing. Dis-ease in the spirit will eventually create disease in the body if you let it stay long enough.

So, I chose peace. Not because what happened did not matter. But because my health, my joy, and my future mattered more than holding onto what was already over.

Now let me talk about something that does not get said enough when we talk about love.

People will decide who you are before they ever really know you.

They will take one piece of your story — one chapter, one moment, one detail — and build an entire verdict around it. And they will deliver that verdict with confidence, like they read the whole book.

I experienced this firsthand.

I remember talking to a guy I dated from Indianapolis. We will call him Indi.

We had been getting to know each other for a while. Good conversation. Building something. And one day we were just talking about our kids — their ages, their personalities, that natural getting-to-know-you kind of conversation. And in the process of talking about how old my son was, he did the math.

He realized I had been a teen mom.

That was all he needed.

Without asking. Without slowing down. Without any curiosity about my story or who I was — the tone shifted. He made assumptions. The kind that let you know exactly what picture someone has already painted without ever picking up a brush.

I checked him. Kindly. But clearly.

I said: you do not know me. You do not know my story. And what you just assumed says a lot more about you than it does about me.

He apologized. For days, actually.

And I want to be clear — that is not why we did not move forward. People misspeak. People make assumptions they later regret. One moment does not have to be the whole verdict. But what that moment revealed was something worth paying attention to.

Some people do not respond to you. They respond to what they think you represent. And if you are not grounded in who you are, you will start believing their version of you over your own.

Your past is not your sentence.

The choices you made in a broken season do not define the woman you have become. And anyone who cannot see past a single chapter to the full story of who you are does not deserve access to your whole heart.

After my marriage ended, I took time.

I poured into my children, my business, my body, my healing. And when I finally opened myself back up — I'm not going to say his name. We'll call him Lifetime.  And I mean that in the most Lifetime movie way possible. The kind of movie where everything on the surface looks almost too perfect to be real.

Because that was him.

He opened doors. Pulled out chairs. Walked on the outside of the sidewalk and pulled me to the inside. Sent flowers. Gifts. Cards with handwritten notes inside them — Dear Candace — once a month. Consistent. Intentional. Present.

It was beautiful.

And I want to be clear — men like that exist. Chivalry is not dead. But something in me kept saying: this is too good to be true.

And people around me said: Candace, you have been with the same person for almost two decades. You are not used to being pursued like this. Open up. Receive it.

So, I started to question myself. Was this fear? Was I holding back because of old pain? Was I about to miss something good because I could not get out of my own way?

Here is what I did not fully understand yet: there is a difference between fear and discernment.

Fear says — run, because you have been hurt before.

Discernment says — pay attention, because something is not aligning.

I silenced my discernment because I thought it was fear.

And then one day, I had a vision. Not something I went looking for. Not something I created. It came to me — clear enough to feel it, specific enough to shake me. And everything I saw eventually came to light.

Everything.

In that moment I had a choice. I could sit in why did this happen to me — or I could stand in what did this teach me.

What it taught me changed how I move forever.

Trust yourself.

Trust your intuition. Trust your discernment. Trust your gift. Because people will talk you out of what your spirit already knows. And that quiet voice inside you — the one that whispers before the evidence shows up — that is not insecurity. That is wisdom.

After Lifetime, I went back to therapy. Not because I was broken. But because I wanted to understand — how did I talk myself out of what I already knew? What needed to be strengthened in me? Because growth requires that kind of honesty.

I gave myself two years before I dated again. And when I stepped back into dating after that, the lesson showed up again. Different situation. Different person. But the same invitation to trust myself.

I was on a date — simple, normal evening. And the guy walked me to the inside of the sidewalk. Pulled me in gently, the way a chivalrous man does.

And instantly my nervous system reacted.

Not because he did anything wrong. But because my body connected it to Lifetime before my mind could catch up.

I had to stop myself right there. Breathe. And remind myself — chivalry still exists. Do not punish this person for what someone else did.

That is what healing looks like in real time. Not perfection. Awareness. Catching yourself before old pain writes a new story about someone who had nothing to do with the old one.

And let me say this about red flags — because we talk about them a lot. But what about yellow flags?

Yellow flags are the ones people sweep under the rug. The small things. The inconsistencies. The moments that make you pause just long enough before you talk yourself out of it.

A yellow flag on its own might not mean much. But enough of them — especially when they keep showing up — start painting a picture. That picture deserves your honest attention even when it does not yet demand your exit.

Do not be so focused on finding love that you stop being honest about what you are actually seeing.

Your discernment is not the enemy of love. It is the protector of it.

One more thing before we close this chapter.

Your happiness is not someone else's responsibility.

That is too much weight to put on anybody. Happiness is a feeling — and feelings change. No person can wake up every single day and make sure you feel whole and at peace. That is your work.

When you rely on someone else to make you happy, you hand them control over your emotional state. And that will have you up one day and down the next based entirely on how they show up. That is not love. That is dependency.

Real love comes from two people who are already doing their own work. Two whole people choosing each other.

At this stage in my life, I do not look for butterflies. I look for peace. I do not look for potential. I look for alignment. And when I think about my future husband, I do not think about perfection. I think about a man who is grounded. A man who has done his work. A man who knows who he is and can meet me where I am — not where I used to be.

A man who loves me — as Ella Mai would say — naked. With all of it. The imperfections, the layers, the full story.

Because who you love matters.

But how you love?

That determines everything.

Before you close this chapter, sit with one question:

Are you loving from wholeness — or from wounds?

You do not have to answer out loud. Just be honest with yourself. Because that answer will tell you everything about what needs to change.

1 Corinthians 13:4-5 — "Love is patient, love is kind. It does not envy, it does not boast, it is not proud. It does not dishonor others, it is not self-seeking."

What this means to me: Real love does not keep score. It does not require you to perform for it. It does not make you feel like you have to earn what should just be given. If the love in your life looks nothing like this description — that is worth paying attention to.

"Stop pouring from empty and calling it love. Fill yourself first. What overflows from a full cup — that's the love worth giving and the love worth receiving."

— *Coach Candace TW*

# I Know My Worth Now

There was a time…
I didn't know how rare I was.
Not really.
I knew I was kind.
I knew I loved deeply.
I knew I gave people chances long after they stopped deserving them.
But knowing your heart…
and knowing your value?
Those are not the same thing.
So, I stayed.
Too long. Too patient. Too understanding.
Too willing to see the good in people
who only saw the good in me when it benefited them.

Men saw my curves before they ever tried to understand my soul.
Saw my softness and mistook it for weakness.
Saw my light…
and thought it was something they could come and go from.
Like it didn't cost me anything to shine.
But light?
Light is not something you borrow.
You either honor it… or you lose it.
And some of them — lost it.

Not because I became bitter.
Not because I hardened my heart.
But because I finally realized…
what I was holding.

See, I am not just beautiful. Beauty fades.

I am not just strong. Strength can be imitated.
No…
I am something deeper than that.
I am a woman who survived things that should have shut her down.
I am the woman who forgave people who never even understood the damage they caused.
I am the woman who kept loving even when love was not returned properly.
The woman who kept building even when life kept knocking the structure down.
And that kind of woman?
She's rare.

Some people wanted my light.
Some people wanted my kindness.
Some people wanted my patience.
Some people wanted the way I poured into them
without ever asking what it cost me.
But wanting a woman…
and knowing how to hold her?
Those are two different conversations.
And some people — never learned the language.

I don't hate them. I don't carry that.
I forgive them.
Even the ones who betrayed me.
Even the ones who lied on me.
Even the ones who used my kindness like it was something they were entitled to…
instead of something they were blessed with.
Even the ones who tried to make me small
because my light made them uncomfortable.
I forgive them.
Not because they deserved it —
but because my peace is too expensive

to be carrying what they did.
And here's the part that makes some people uncomfortable.
I'm not the same woman anymore.
Not the one who stayed quiet.
Not the one who waited to be chosen.
Not the one who kept shrinking so other people could feel bigger.
No.
This woman?
This woman knows her worth.

She knows that every curve on her body was placed there on purpose.
That every scar on her heart taught her something.
That every betrayal trained her discernment.
That every season of starting over was not failure —
it was refinement.

So now?
Now when someone meets me,
they don't meet the woman who didn't know her value.
They meet the woman who finally does.

And when the men who knew me before see me now…
they'll understand something.
Not through anger.
Not through bitterness.
Just truth.
They had something rare in their hands…
and they didn't know how to hold it.
And that's okay.
Because the lesson was never about proving them wrong.
The lesson…
was about finally understanding
I was never the one who needed fixing.

## CHAPTER 6

# Speaking Life When Life Is Loud

"Your words are seeds. Be careful what you plant — because you will eventually live in what grows."

— *Coach Candace TW*

My grandma used to get on the bus every single morning and say it out loud.

To nobody in particular. To everybody at the same time.

This is the day the Lord has made. We will rejoice and be glad in it.

Every morning. Without fail.

And I will be honest with you — as a kid, I was embarrassed. I would sit there hoping nobody I knew was on that bus. Hoping she would not say it too loud. Hoping we could just ride in peace like normal people.

My grandma was not concerned with any of that.

She was setting the tone for her day before her day had a chance to set it for her.

I did not understand that then.

I understand it completely now.

Dorothy J. — I love you. I miss you. Thank you for every lesson you did not even know you were teaching me.

Life has a way of getting loud.

Not the good kind — not music, laughter, or celebration.

The other kind.

Bills stacking.

Relationships straining.

Plans unraveling right in your hands while you are still holding them.

And when life gets loud like that, your mind starts talking back.

Sometimes it whispers.

Sometimes it screams.

Why is this happening?

When does it change?

Is this just how it is now?

If you are not careful, those thoughts become words. And words — once they leave your mouth — are no longer just thoughts.

They are seeds.

The Bible says death and life are in the power of the tongue. Not sometimes. Not in extreme cases. The full weight of both outcomes lives right there in what you choose to say. That is not just a spiritual principle — science confirms it too.

Your brain has something called a reticular activating system — essentially a filter that directs your attention toward whatever you have told it matters. Here is a simple way to understand it: have you ever gotten a new car — specific make, specific model, specific color — and suddenly that exact car was everywhere on the road? Those cars were always there. You just were not looking for them. The moment that car became yours, your brain started spotting it everywhere.

Speaking life works the same way.

When you start saying I am healing, I am building, I am moving toward something better — your brain begins finding evidence for it. Opportunities that were already there become visible. The right people start showing up. Doors you never noticed begin to open.

Not because the words did the work.

Because the words changed what you were looking for.

And what you look for, you find.

Now let me be clear about something — because I am a coach and I do not do delusion.

Speaking life is not sitting on a couch making declarations while the work does not get done.

Faith without work is dead. You speak it, write it down, put it on the vision board, build the plan — and then you get up and you move toward it. The words create the posture. The posture fuels the belief. The belief drives the action. The action produces the results.

You cannot skip the doing and expect the speaking to carry you.

What changes when you shift your words is not that the work disappears. It is that you show up for the work differently. With expectation instead of dread. With belief instead of defeat.

I teach this from the very first consultation.

In my sessions, we do not speak against ourselves. I have had people push back — but Coach Candace, I know what I look like. And I hear that. They do know. That is exactly why they showed up. They made a decision to change. They could have spent that money on shoes, on a bag, on anything else — but they invested in their health instead. We are not spending our sessions rehearsing where we started. We are speaking to where we are going.

We do not use the word fat in my space. Not because we are ignoring reality, but because that is not our destination.

From day one, I set the standard: we do not say I can't in here. What we say is — I can. I will. I must.

That is a chant I learned from motivational speaker Eric Thomas, and it became something we live by. When the exercise gets hard, when life gets hard, when everything in you wants to quit — that is what you say out loud. I can. I will. I must. You say it until your body catches up with what your mouth already declared. Because it will.

This is what I mean when I say transform your mind, transform your body. It does not start in the gym. It starts in the language you use about yourself every single day.

The client who starts declaring I am getting stronger, I am leaning out, I am becoming — before the mirror confirms it, before anyone else notices — gets there faster. Not because the words did the squats for her. Because the words changed how she showed up for the squats.

That is not a fitness principle. That is a life principle.

Now let us talk about what we say to each other — because this needs to be addressed too.

Jokes have teeth.

I know people who say something cutting and then say I'm just joking — and then repeat the same thing again. What I have had to learn, and remind others, is that your intention does not change where the words land. The spirit does not sort what was meant to be funny from what was meant to wound. They go out the same.

When you tell someone — even laughing — you're so slow, you can't get anything right, you're a klutz — those words file somewhere. In a child, they file fast and they file deep.

My mom used to say to me, joking: Candace, you can't walk and chew bubblegum at the same time. She meant nothing by it. Said it maybe a handful of times total. But I started repeating it to myself as an adult without even realizing I was doing it. I would catch myself saying it like it was just fact.

And then I actually did some research and found out the brain is not optimally built for multitasking anyway. When you split your focus three ways, nothing gets a hundred percent. Sometimes what looked like a limitation was actually a feature. I could not wait to tell her that. We laughed about it. But the point stands: the word had already gotten comfortable enough in my mind to feel like truth. That is how subtle this is.

My oldest son was labeled early.

He can't sit still. He's bad. He's a behavior problem.

I refused to let that stick. He is not bad — he is busy. There is a difference.

His kindergarten teacher, Miss Willis from Leif Erikson, saw it too. She refused to put him on medication when the system was pushing for it. She said: we are going to work with him. She created a plan. She stayed.

And that boy — the one they wanted to write off in kindergarten — was tutoring seniors in math as a freshman in high school. A freshman. Whatever lesson you put in front of him, he had it in seconds. Every sport he touched, he was gifted. Coaches used to say they had never seen anything like it.

Scouts were paying attention.

But then a teacher — not meaning harm, genuinely believing he was being real with him — planted something different.

He told my son that thousands of kids — thousands of little Black boys — were all going after the same dream. That the odds were stacked. That he needed a realistic backup plan.

My son came home and said: Mom, my teacher said I might not make it because everybody's going for the same thing.

And I told him: What that means is you have to want it more than everybody else. While they are sleeping, you are training. While they are comfortable, you are hungry. You speak it over your life — and then you do the work to back it up.

He kept showing up. He kept working. Scouts kept coming.

Then there was an altercation.

He did not start it. He was defending himself. And both young men were disciplined — though my son received fewer days than the other student. But the rule was clear: any suspension meant you did not play.

He was supposed to suit up and sit on the bench. Be present even if he could not be on the field. Scouts were in those stands that day.

He chose not to go. He was not happy he couldn't play.

And when I asked him why —

There's a thousand of us going for the same thing anyway. So it's alright.

There it was.

That one sentence. Said by a teacher who never thought about that conversation again. Filed away quietly in my son's spirit. Sitting there. Waiting. And when the moment came that required him to fight for his dream —

those words were louder than his belief.

That is what planted words do.

They do not always surface immediately. Sometimes they wait for the moment when you are most vulnerable — when the excuse presents itself — and then they hand you a reason to stop.

Be careful what you plant in people. Especially young people who are still deciding what they believe about themselves.

Your words — said once, said casually, said without any bad intention at all — can still take root and grow long after you have forgotten you said them.

Speak to who people are becoming.

Not just to where they are.

Now, complaining.

There is a difference between processing something hard and rehearsing it.

I will listen. I will be a shoulder. I will sit with you in it. But after a certain point — as a friend, as a coach, as someone who loves you — the real question has to be asked: So, what are you going to do about it?

Because if every call, every morning, every conversation opens the same way — same problem, same spiral, same story replaying — you are not processing anymore. You are rehearsing. You are giving that problem the stage every single day. You are amplifying it. You are making it louder than it needs to be because repetition gives things weight.

And here is what that does over time: it makes the problem feel permanent. It starts to feel like this is just how it is. Your identity starts to wrap around the struggle instead of the solution.

Enter His gates with thanksgiving and His courts with praise. Not because everything is fine. Because gratitude shifts your focus — and focus determines what you are moving toward.

Write the plan. Speak to the solution. Take one step, then the next. That is how the trajectory changes. Not in one dramatic moment. In the daily, quiet decision to stop rehearsing the problem and start declaring the way through it.

Now let me tell you a story.

I was eighteen. On my own. My first apartment. My son and I.

His father and I were done — I had asked him to leave, and he left. That was the right call. We had good times. He introduced me to things in life I had never experienced. But over time, the compound effect of the unpleasant times — the things that were not healthy, the things that were not safe — those things added up. And they were not worth staying for.

We are actually friends now. We can talk, laugh, share stories about our grandchildren. And I am grateful for that. But at that time, leaving was the right decision.

When he left, the budget changed fast. And he did not just leave — he left damage behind that had to be dealt with. Broken things. Money gone. A gap where stability used to be.

I want to be clear about something, because I know how this sounds: I have always been smart with money. Even at eighteen.

My rule was simple — if I did not have two to three times the amount saved up, I was not spending it. But when the budget changes and things break and Christmas is coming and the refrigerator is running low — it does not matter how disciplined you are. The math was hard.

And Christmas was coming.

Now, I know what some people are going to say. I know there are people who call Christmas a pagan holiday, who know the history, who do not celebrate it for their own reasons — and I respect all of that. I understand the history. I am not arguing with you about the origins.

What I know is this: my son was little. And I wanted him to have that morning. The imagination. The magic. The memory of waking up and seeing something waiting for him under that tree. To me, in that season, that mattered. That was worth fighting for.

So I was down. But I was not defeated.

Because even at eighteen, even before I had language for manifestation or understood what scripture said about the power of words, I had always believed — in my bones, since I was a little girl — that if you say it and mean it, it can happen. So every day, multiple times a day, I said it out loud:

This too shall pass.

Over and over. Day after day. Until those words became the soundtrack running underneath everything else.

My car had been repossessed by this point. That is how tight things had gotten. So, I called my son's father and asked if he could drive us to my mom's house. She had cooked a meal and had some food set aside for us — that was why we were originally going. I did not want to call him. He was petty, and there was a part of him that took quiet satisfaction in watching me struggle after I put him out. But it was cold. My son was with me. Pride does not keep a child warm.

He called to say he was outside.

I bundled my son up. I opened the front door to walk out.

Two women were standing on my porch.

Two female postal workers — standing right there, about to ring my doorbell, holding a letter in their hands.

My letter.

The Santa Claus letter.

Earlier that year, through a support program for young mothers inside Marshall High School — a program meant to help us stay in school, stay supported, keep going — we had done an activity with our kids. Writing letters to Santa Claus. A small thing. A fun afternoon. I sent the letter and forgot it existed.

Those women had not forgotten.

They came to my door, in the cold, in the middle of December, to be my Santa Claus.

I started crying immediately after they explained why they were there.

Right there. On my doorstep. Before we went anywhere.

I told them — I am literally about to leave right now to go get food. We do not have food. That is my son's father outside. And here you are. Right now. At this exact moment.

They looked at each other.

Do you want us to take you?

I crouched down to eye level with my son and told his father to go. He pulled off.

Those two women took us to the grocery store and filled the cart. They took my son to pick out his own toys and let him choose every one. They put money in my pocket. They gave me a gift card. They took us to my mom's house so I could pick up the meal she had waiting — and my mom, who is not a crier, who keeps her emotions close and her strength tight, was genuinely happy. She thanked them with everything she had. You could see the gratitude shine across her face, even though she was not falling apart. That is just who she is — joy without tears.

Then those women took us back home. Helped get everything inside.

They did not have to do any of that.

Christmas morning, my son woke up to gifts under the tree and food in the kitchen.

And I have never forgotten.

One of the ladies said something I carry to this day: God hears you. He uses people. He is always right on time.

I had completely forgotten I wrote that letter. It was just an afternoon activity. Just a piece of paper. But somewhere between writing it and that doorstep, what I forgot became the provision I never saw coming.

Message.

I had no idea how it was going to work out. I did not know what form the answer would take. I just kept saying this too shall pass and kept living like it was already true.

And it was.

That is how this works. You do not always get to see the how. You keep speaking. You keep believing. You keep moving. And what was already in motion finds you.

But that was not the only time I had to fight to stay here. I am about to share something I have never shared publicly before…

Something I carried in silence for years.

And I am sharing it now — not because it is easy, but because I know someone reading this needs to hear it. And I have healed enough to tell it. I cry as I write this — not from pain, but from gratitude. Not because the memory is still open. Because the testimony is bigger than the pain.

There was a season in my life where the weight of everything became too much.

Not a moment. A season.

A season where the noise got so loud — the weight of everything I had survived, everything I was still carrying, everything I was trying to hold together in my marriage while quietly falling apart — that I got to a place I never imagined I would get to.

A place where the voice inside me stopped speaking life altogether.

I was not weak. I was not faithless. I was human. And I was exhausted in a way that went deeper than tired.

From the outside, nobody would have known. I was on autopilot. I got up every day. I cooked for my family. Got my kids ready. Dropped them off at school.

And then I came home and sat on the couch.

And repeated it the next day.

My kids always had my love — that never wavered. But I was not there the way I needed to be. I was moving. I was functioning. But something inside me had gone very, very quiet.

And somewhere in that quiet, a voice started speaking.

They would be better off without you.

I want you to understand something about that voice. It does not announce itself. It does not come in loud and dramatic. It slides in. It sounds almost logical. Almost reasonable. And if you are exhausted enough, depleted enough, disconnected enough from the truth of who you are — it starts to sound like the truth.

I stopped going outside. I stopped engaging the way I normally would. My cousin was the only person who noticed. She would later share with me that she felt something was wrong even though I had not said a word. She told me she would cry because she did not know how to help. I did not tell her until months later. I did not tell anyone.

I wrote a letter.

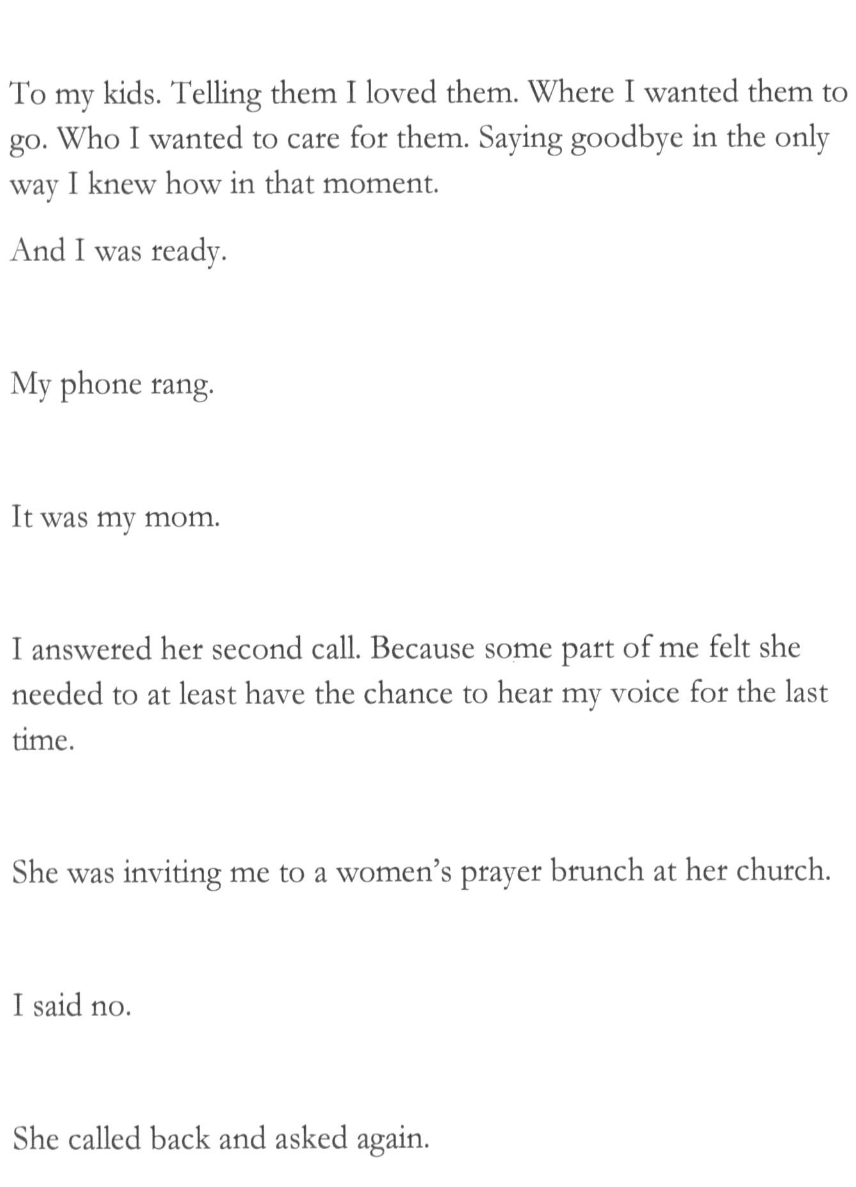

To my kids. Telling them I loved them. Where I wanted them to go. Who I wanted to care for them. Saying goodbye in the only way I knew how in that moment.

And I was ready.

My phone rang.

It was my mom.

I answered her second call. Because some part of me felt she needed to at least have the chance to hear my voice for the last time.

She was inviting me to a women's prayer brunch at her church.

I said no.

She called back and asked again.

And something in me said — this will be the last time she gets to see me. Just go. When you come back, you can still do it. Just go.

So, I went.

I sat near the back. I was not there to receive anything. I was not there to stay. I was there because my mother's voice had reached something in me that I could not explain, and I had made a bargain with myself that I did not fully understand yet.

One of the speakers said something that landed on me like it was spoken directly into my chest:

You are not here today because of you. God used someone to get you here. There is a reason you are in this room today.

I sat with that. And I would understand why later — after what happened next.

Then came the prayer portion. They were calling people up. I stayed in my seat. I was not going up there. I had already decided what I was going home to do.

And then the woman who had been speaking walked back to where I was sitting.

She reached out her hand.

You. Get up here. Let me pray for you.

She pulled me forward. She wrapped her arms around me. And she leaned in close and whispered something in my ear that stopped my entire world.

You shall live and not die.

And then she began to speak things over me — things that I had been saying to myself in the mirror that very morning. Private things. Things nobody in that room could have known. Things I had never spoken out loud to another person.

She told me why I needed to live.

She told me what I was carrying that I needed to put down.

She told me I had a purpose.

And I cried.

The tears would not stop coming, even after I went back to my seat. Baby, I cried the way a person cries when something that has been locked inside for too long finally breaks free.

My mom was in that room. She did not know what was happening. Nobody did. Nobody knew what I had written that morning, what I had planned, what I had almost done.

But God knew.

And He sent my mother to call me.

And He sent those words to land on me.

And He sent that woman to find me in the back of that room and speak life over me when I had run completely out of life to speak over myself.

That day, I chose to live.

Not just to survive. To live. On purpose. Intentionally. From that day forward, everything I did had to mean something. Had to have purpose. Had to point somewhere.

I found my voice.

And things started to shift.

I carried that testimony in silence for years.

I was embarrassed by it.

I had associated weakness with what I had gone through. Cowardice, even. That is what I told myself. And I was afraid of what people would think — how could someone who looks so strong have been that broken? How could a mom even get to that place?

But that is exactly why I am telling you.

Because strength is not the absence of breaking.

Strength is what happens when you break all the way down — and then you choose, one more time, to get back up.

What I want you to take from this is not the details.

It is this:

You are not weak for having been in a dark place.

You are human.

And if you are in that place right now — if you are sitting somewhere reading this and the voice in your head is saying things that sound like what I described — please hear me:

You are not alone.

You are not a burden.

You are not better off gone.

Get help. Talk to someone. Reach out to a crisis line. Let someone in. Because the voice that tells you to stay silent is the same voice that wants to win.

Do not let it win.

You shall live and not die.

Say it. Believe it. Hold onto it with everything you have until you can feel it in your bones.

And if you cannot feel it yet — borrow mine until you can.

I still say this too shall pass.

Even now. Even in seasons that people around me do not even know I am in — because I learned how to wear a face when I needed to. My person, my friends, my family — sometimes none of them know what I am carrying. And I chant it quietly, privately, until the pressure shifts.

And it always shifts.

The opportunities show up. The right person reaches out. The door opens from a direction you were not even looking at. Not because you made it happen. Because you kept speaking it, kept believing it, kept showing up as if it was already done.

I can. I will. I must.

That is not a motivational poster. That is a survival tool. That is what got me through workouts I wanted to quit. It is what got me through seasons I wanted to surrender. And it is what I pour into every person who walks into my space — because the words that carried me are the same words that can carry them.

This is why I am not just a fitness trainer.

The body work and the mind work are the same work. You cannot separate them. The language you use about yourself shows up in the choices you make, the weight you carry, the relationships you accept, the opportunities you reach for. All of it is connected. And when people find their way to me — whether through a class, a challenge, a voice note, a social media post — they come thinking they need the physical. And they do. But there is usually something more they needed to hear.

That is my ministry. It always has been.

And this book is part of it.

Wherever you are right now — whatever has been loud in your life lately — here is what I need you to hear:

Change the words.

Not as performance. Not as pretending everything is fine when it is not. But as a declaration of where you are headed, even when where you are right now is hard.

Write it down. Say it out loud. Put it somewhere you will see it every single day. And then do the work to match what your mouth is already declaring.

This too shall pass.

I can. I will. I must.

Start there. And don't stop.

Before you leave this chapter:

Write down three things you have been speaking over your life — out loud or in your head — that need to change. Then write the truth beneath each one. Not what the situation looks like right now. What you are believing for.

Speak that instead. Every day. Until it becomes the loudest voice in the room.

Proverbs 18:21 — "Death and life are in the power of the tongue, and those who love it will eat its fruit."

What this means to me: You are eating the fruit of what you have been speaking. If you do not like what is on the table, it is time to plant something different. It is never too late to change what you are growing.

"The words you speak over your life today are the seeds of the harvest you'll walk into tomorrow. Choose them like your future depends on it — because it does."— *Coach Candace TW*

If you or someone you know is struggling, please reach out. You do not have to carry it alone.

National Suicide Prevention Lifeline: 988

Crisis Text Line: Text HOME to 741741

# CHAPTER 7

# Even the Motivator Needs Motivation

"You cannot pour from an empty cup. And you cannot keep running on fumes and call it strength. At some point, rest is not a reward — it is a requirement."

— *Coach Candace TW*

People often assume the person doing the motivating must always be motivated.

They see the energy.

They hear the words.

They watch the consistency.

And they think: she must never get tired.

That is not how life works.

Even the motivator needs motivation.

Even the one pouring into everyone else has moments where her own cup feels low. Even the strong friend, the coach, the encourager, the one people lean on — still has days where she needs someone to lean on too.

Not every day.

But enough days to remind you that you are still human.

As a coach, people see me in one role.

The motivator.

The one pushing the room.

The one saying — you can do this, don't quit now, you are stronger than you think.

They see the consistency.

What they do not always see is what happens after the room empties.

When the coach has to sit down and pour back into herself.

There are days when my body is tired.

Not lazy tired. Life tired.

The kind of tired that builds quietly underneath all the showing up. The kind that does not announce itself until one day your body speaks up and says — enough.

And on those days, there is only one right response:

Practice what you preach.

Before I became a trainer, before any of this existed, there was a season when I was carrying more than I knew how to hold.

Still married. Still living a life that looked one way from the outside and felt entirely different on the inside. Going to work, coming home, cooking, cleaning, raising my children, trying to hold everything together while quietly falling apart.

I was showing up for everyone else.

I was disappearing inside myself.

Eventually, I ended up in the hospital from anxiety attacks. Later, I had to take medical leave from work — not for something you could see, but for the weight of everything I had been absorbing in silence.

There was clinical language for it.

What it really was, simply, was this:

I had been pushing through so much for so long, in silence, that my body finally said enough.

Then I developed a nerve condition.

That was the moment I stopped arguing with what my body was trying to tell me.

Your body keeps score.

That is not just a saying. That is science.

When you carry chronic stress without release, without recovery, without ever allowing yourself to fully come down — your body produces cortisol at levels it was never designed to sustain.

It disrupts sleep.

It affects weight, immunity, hormones, mood, and memory.

It keeps your nervous system in a state of low-grade emergency even when no emergency is present.

Dis-ease in the body.

And dis-ease, held long enough, creates disease.

I know this from studying it.

I know this from teaching it.

And I know it because I lived it before I even had the language for it.

Message.

Therapy was part of how I started to understand what my body had been trying to tell me for years.

I want to speak directly to this — especially to my community — because there is still too much silence around it.

Going to therapy does not mean your faith is not strong enough. It does not mean you are weak or broken. It means you are wise enough to know that some things need a trained professional — in a room where none of your masks are allowed.

I went.

I sat.

I told the truth.

And in that room, connections got made that I could not have made alone. Patterns became visible. I began to understand not just what I had been through, but how it had been living quietly in my body, my choices, and my relationships — shaping things underneath the surface that I did not even know were being shaped.

Choosing therapy is not always about falling apart.

Sometimes it is about getting the tools. About becoming better equipped for life before things reach a breaking point.

Not breakdown.

Preparation.

I went to therapy more than once. Each time, it gave me something I needed — clarity, tools, and permission to see myself honestly without judgment.

Each time, I came out better equipped than I went in.

You deserve that too.

Not just enough healing to keep functioning.

All-the-way healed.

The kind of healed where you can sit in a quiet room and not be afraid of what surfaces.

There is a motivational speech I come back to — the kind you find when you search for something that speaks to exactly where you are.

The message is simple, and it is true:

It is just you versus your mind. Every single day.

That is the real battle.

Not the circumstances.

Not the people who did not show up.

Not the doors that closed.

The battle is in your head.

In the story you are telling yourself about what is happening.

In whether you let exhaustion convince you it is over when it is not.

In whether you mistake stillness for failure when it is actually recovery.

The motivator is not exempt from that battle.

I have been in some of my hardest seasons, and nobody knew. I kept posting. I kept coaching. I kept showing up — not to perform, but because I had learned how to speak life even from the dark.

And speaking it helped pull me through.

Before you can pour into anyone else, you have to remember why you started.

Don't forget how badly you once wanted what you now have.

The clients. The platform. The trust. The access to people's lives at their most vulnerable moments. The room that fills up because of something you built from nothing, from faith, from refusing to quit when quitting would have been easier.

That desire was the seed.

Rest is how you protect the harvest.

Because you cannot build something lasting while running on empty. And the people who need what you carry deserve the full version of you — not the depleted version showing up on autopilot.

At one point, I made a decision.

I was going to take a pause-cation.

I cleared my schedule in advance. I let my clients and my challenge members know. I put it out there honestly:

Coach is taking a pause. It is time for me to listen to myself for a while.

Phone on Do Not Disturb. Schedule cleared. Permission given — by me, to me — to be still.

Then the first morning of my pause-cation came.

My body woke me up at four in the morning. Because that is what it knows. That is the time I usually get up for early class — to show up, to pour out. My body had its routine.

And my body did not know we were resting.

I laid there and had to tell myself: girl, lay back down.

I went back to sleep. Woke up later than I had in a long time. And sat with the strangest feeling.

Guilt.

Not because anything was wrong.

Because nothing was happening.

Because I was not moving, not helping, not pouring into anyone. And I am so used to doing all of those things that the absence of them felt like failure. Like I was not doing my due diligence. Like somewhere out there someone needed me and I was just —

still.

I had to have a real conversation with myself.

Sit down.

You do not have to move right now.

You do not have to help anyone.

You gave them the tools.

You sent the videos.

You sent the emails.

You told them you were pausing.

Now pause.

Movement does not equal productivity. Being busy does not mean you are building. You can run from sunrise to midnight and still be running away from the very thing you actually need.

Rest.

That day, I had to put down the plates.

If you have ever seen the image of a woman balancing plates on both arms, one on her head, somehow still reaching to pick up what someone else dropped —

that was me.

That had been me for years.

Mom.

Coach.

Entrepreneur.

Friend.

Partner.

Daughter.

Community.

All of it balanced.

None of it ever fully set down.

The pause-cation was the first time I gave myself permission to let the plates rest on the table.

Even after I told people I was pausing — and I say this with nothing but love because these people genuinely care about me — some of them kept reaching out.

Fitness questions.

Supplement questions.

Check-ins that turned into full conversations.

People texting my personal line about business because they had access and were used to having access.

So I had to set a boundary. Kindly. But clearly.

When a business closes for the holidays, you do not stand at the door expecting them to open it just for you. You wait. You use the resources already available. You respect that there are hours — and the people inside are allowed to close.

I am a person.

I am also a business.

And I told everyone I was closed.

If you care about someone who tells you they are resting, the most loving thing you can do is let them rest.

Not call to check if they are available.

Not reach out because you saw them post a photo.

Not treat the pause as optional for everyone except you.

Give me the grace of my own pause-cation.

Because here is the truth: you cannot give your best to people running on ten percent. You cannot inspire from a place of depletion.

The tools I gave my clients, the messages I sent, the emails I prepared before I stepped away — those came from a version of me that had poured out and poured out and poured out.

The pause was so I could return as the version of me who had something real to give again.

Something I once shared with a friend during that season is worth repeating here, because someone reading this might need it too:

I know you said I can call on you anytime. But I am not always going to unload on you like that. Your peace matters just as much as mine. Your health matters just as much as mine.

Sometimes I will figure things out myself first. Sometimes I will pray. Sometimes I will sit in silence. Sometimes I will cry, journal, meditate, talk to God, or just be still. And when I do share, it might be once I have some clarity or testimony behind it.

That is not distance.

That is wisdom.

Because sometimes you do not need advice. You do not need noise from the outside. You do not need someone else's perspective layered on top of what you are already carrying.

You just need stillness long enough to hear the answer.

Movement is healthy.

But stillness is healthy too.

Learning to tell the difference — learning to sit in quiet without guilt, without the feeling that you are failing someone — is one of the most important things I have had to teach myself.

Something beautiful happens when you pour into people genuinely over years.

Eventually, some of it comes back.

At a bodybuilding show, a woman walked up to me and told me what my presence had meant to her. She had been watching since the early days. She said: because of you, I did this.

She competed not for the aesthetics, but to prove something to herself. To be an example for her son. When she wanted to quit, she heard my voice in her head.

I had been posting into what sometimes felt like silence. Four people watching some days. Wondering if any of it was landing.

And there she was — telling me it had not just landed. It had grown into something she carried into her hardest moments.

That moment motivated me more than I had motivated her that day.

Because she reminded me that even in the seasons when I was exhausted, even when I was in the dark behind the smile —

The seeds were still growing in places I could not see.

That same truth showed up again at my high school alumni picnic. People I had not seen in years walked up to tell me I had inspired them. People who never liked a post, never left a comment, never made themselves visible — but they had been watching. Something I said — something about the way I kept showing up — had mattered to them.

You never know who is watching.

You never know which word, which moment, which act of you simply continuing to show up is changing something in someone you cannot see.

That is why you keep planting even when you cannot see the harvest.

That is why you rest — so you can keep planting.

So, if you are the strong one — the encourager, the motivator, the one people lean on — hear this:

You are allowed to be tired.

You are allowed to need encouragement too.

You are allowed to close the door, refill the cup, sit in the stillness, and feel no guilt about it.

Take care of your body.

Move.

Eat clean.

But also protect your peace.

Sometimes the strongest thing you can do is pause, breathe, and reset — not because you are giving up, but because you are gearing up.

The world does not need you burned out.

The world needs you whole.

And sometimes the most powerful thing a motivator can do is pause long enough to remember —

she deserves motivation too.

Starting with herself.

Matthew 11:28 — "Come to me, all you who are weary and burdened, and I will give you rest."

What this means to me: He did not say come when the list is done. He did not say come when you have it together. He said come as you are — weary, burdened, running on empty — and I will give you rest. That is a promise. And I have held onto it in more seasons than I can count.

"Even the motivator needs motivation. Even the strong need someone to speak life over them. Even the person who shows up for everyone else deserves to have someone show up for her — starting with herself."

— *Coach Candace TW*

## Somewhere Between the Storm

I learned something about storms.

They don't always announce themselves.

They don't always come loud
with thunder cracking the sky
so you can brace yourself.

No…

Sometimes they slip in quiet.

Like a shadow
moving across the room.

One day you standing strong…

and the next—

you carrying mountains
in your chest…

and nobody sees
the weight.

People still smiling at you.

Still saying,
"How you doing?"

And you?

You say,

"I'm good."

Because strong women learn early…

how to hold earthquakes
behind steady voices.

I smiled through storms
with rain sitting heavy in my chest.

Walked into rooms
with lightning in my bones.

Kept pouring light into people…

while secretly praying
somebody—

anybody—

would notice
my candle
was burning low.

But life?

Life kept life'n.
Didn't slow down.
Didn't check on me.
Didn't ask if I needed a minute.

Dreams bent in the wind.

Plans scattered
like loose papers
on a city street.

Some nights…

my faith was barely a whisper.

Some mornings…

I woke up tired
before the day even started.

But here's the thing
about women who pray…

Even when we tired—

we still show up.

Even when the road looks empty—

we still walk it.

Even when the answers don't come—

we still believe
they somewhere out there
waiting on us to meet them.

And somewhere between…

the crying…

and the continuing…

something in me—

something deep—

refused to quit.

Not loud.

Not dramatic.

Just a stubborn kind of hope…

sitting low in my spirit
like a whisper that wouldn't leave me alone:

"You're not done yet."

So I kept going.

Kept building.

Kept planting seeds
in seasons
that looked like drought.

Kept watering dreams
nobody else could see growing.

Because sometimes faith…

isn't loud.

It ain't always hands lifted
and voices raised.

Sometimes faith…

is sitting in the dark…

talking to yourself…

trying to hold it together…

and whispering—

"Just make it to tomorrow."

And I did.

Tomorrow came. Then another one. Then another one.

And somewhere along the way…

the same storm
that tried to drown me…

started teaching me
how to swim.

So no—

I didn't become fearless.

I became faithful.

Faithful enough
to keep standing.

Faithful enough
to keep walking.

Faithful enough
to trust that the same God
who carried me through yesterday…

was already standing
inside tomorrow…

waiting on me
to show up.

And I did.

Still breathing.
Still believing.

Still becoming.

Somewhere between the storm…

and the woman I am now—

I found out
I was stronger than the storm
ever expected me to be.

# CHAPTER 8

## What I Did Wrong and What I Didn't

"Growth requires honesty. Not the kind that tears you down, but the kind that tells the truth so you can grow wiser."

— *Coach Candace TW*

By the time you finish this chapter, the poem that follows will hit differently.

Everything that follows is just me telling you the full story.

One of the greatest teachers in my life has been motherhood.

Nothing will show you your strengths and your weaknesses faster than raising children. And when I look back over the years, there are things I know I did wrong. There are also things I know I did right.

Both can be true at the same time.

People sometimes think parenting is about getting everything perfect. It is not. Parenting is about loving your children enough to keep learning as you go — and being honest enough with yourself to admit when you missed something, even when admitting it is uncomfortable.

My children have taught me resilience in ways no classroom ever could.

Let me start with the one who started it all.

He was due at the end of July. My birthday is July 14th, and I held onto that. I was already carrying the weight of being a teen mom, but I told myself — at least I will be sixteen. At least there is that.

He came July 9th.

Five days before my birthday. I was still fifteen.

So when people ask, I say sixteen. Five days felt like it should have counted for something. But this book is built on truth, and the truth is I was fifteen years old when Ronnie came into the world.

A child raising a child.

The moment I found out I was pregnant, something in me shifted. I ordered books on healthy pregnancies and new motherhood, and I applied what I learned — before he arrived and after. I read to him when he was little. Had real conversations with him. I wanted him to have the best shot, and I understood even then that giving him that started with me doing the work.

Whenever I stepped into something new, that is what I did.

I studied. I prepared. I showed up.

And yet — I have to be honest about where I was before he arrived.

I talked in an earlier chapter about the dark season I had been living in. I had been ditching school more than I should have, following behind Ronnie's father, who had dropped out of school himself, being rebellious when what I needed was direction. Before things went dark, I had been a good student. Then the hurt took over and the focus got blurry.

When Ronnie arrived, the blurriness cleared.

I had to get back on track — not just for him, but for both of us. He gave me back my direction when I had been losing it. He made me want to show up differently, dream again, build something worth showing him.

He saved me in ways he will probably never fully understand.

Which is why this chapter has to begin with him. Not to put him on trial. Not to air anything that does not need to be aired. But because when he reads this, I need him to feel exactly one thing:

Loved. Prayed over. Believed in.

Always.

Ronnie was something from the beginning.

Whatever lesson you put in front of him, he absorbed it fast. As a freshman in high school, he was tutoring seniors in math. A freshman. Tutoring seniors. His mind worked like that — quick, sharp, always moving forward.

And then there was the speed.

This boy could run. The kind of fast that makes people stop what they are doing and look twice. He played every sport — baseball, football, basketball, track — and what stood out was not just that he was athletic. It was that he was genuinely gifted at every single one. Coaches noticed. Scouts noticed. Every season, every field — he showed up and he delivered.

Getting to that point, though, took some navigating.

In kindergarten, they called it a behavior problem. They said he was bad.

I said he was busy. There is a difference.

His kindergarten teacher, Miss Willis, understood that difference. When I requested an evaluation — because I was not about to let anyone label my son as a problem and move on — the results came back with a diagnosis of ADHD. And when the suggestion was made to put him on medication, Miss Willis said no.

She said: I will work with him.

She built a plan around who he actually was instead of who he was inconveniencing. She saw my son when it would have been easier to just manage him.

I will always be grateful for that woman.

What I know is this: a child who cannot sit still is not broken. A child who cannot be contained is not a problem. Sometimes that child just needs an outlet worthy of his energy. We kept Ronnie in sports. We kept him active, structured, and pointed toward something positive.

When he had that, he thrived.

When he did not — he found something else to fill the space.

That is not his fault. That is how brilliance without direction works. And as his mother, I have to own the parts where the direction I provided was not always enough.

There was a teacher who said something I believe planted a seed I wish had never taken root.

This teacher was not trying to harm him. The intention was preparation. He told my son that thousands of kids — thousands of little Black boys — were all chasing the same dream of going pro. That the odds were stacked. That he needed a backup plan.

Ronnie came home and told me.

I told him: that means you have to want it more than everybody else. While they sleep, you train. While they get comfortable, you stay hungry. You speak it over your life — and then you do the work to back it up.

He heard me. He kept showing up. Scouts were paying attention.

Then came an incident that was not his fault — self-defense, the kind of thing that happens when you are a young man in a moment you did not ask for. Both kids were disciplined. The rule was clear: suspension meant sitting out a game. This particular game, scouts were in the stands.

He was not there.

And the excuse he found to make peace with stepping back traced right to that planted word.

It is a thousand of us going for the same thing anyway.

Those words had been waiting for a moment of disappointment to attach to.

They found one.

Be careful what you plant in young people. Words do not disappear. They root. They wait. And they surface when the timing is most costly.

Ronnie eventually stepped into his own life. He felt grown, decided he did not want to follow the rules anymore, and stepped out. And I had to learn what most mothers of sons eventually learn — there is a point where you cannot hold them. You can only love them, pray over them, and trust what you planted to eventually surface.

That is one of the hardest things I have ever had to do.

Watch your child move through choices you do not understand. Love him completely through all of it without being able to fix it. Show up for him every time, even when it hurts, even when you are on your knees asking God to cover what you cannot reach.

I pray for Ronnie the way I breathe.

Consistently. Quietly. Without stopping.

I hold onto the scripture that says if you train up a child in the way he should go, even when he strays, he will come back to it. Some days that scripture is the only thing that quiets the worry.

Because this boy is smart, funny, loyal, and full of more potential than he is currently using. I have videos of Ronnie that crack me up every time. His humor. The way he loves his siblings. How he showed up when Laniyah went off to her first year of college — rearranged his schedule to make sure she had what she needed, showed up with her refrigerator, played every game at her trunk party.

That is who Ronnie is underneath everything else.

He still checks on me. I still check on him. Sometimes it is just a text. Sometimes just I love you. But it is never nothing.

There is something I cannot fully explain but have never doubted. I can feel when something is off with my children. Even now, even with Ronnie grown and living his own life, if something is wrong, I know before he says a word. I will reach out and he will say: Mom, how did you know?

I just know.

Whether that is a mother's intuition or something deeper, I cannot say. What I know is that the connection between us has never broken. Not through the hard seasons. Not through any of it.

Ronnie, if you are reading this:

This is your mama. Correcting you with love because that is the only way I know how. I do not agree with every choice you are making. I do not understand every road you are walking. But I have never stopped believing in who you are capable of becoming.

You are prayed over. You are loved. You are mine.

And your story is not finished. Not even close.

My only daughter, Laniyah — we call her Niyah — showed me what resilience actually looks like up close.

She started having seizures at thirteen months old. They came often, they came hard, and they continued through her childhood. Any parent who has watched their child go through something like that knows the feeling. Your heart drops in ways words cannot fully explain. Hospital visits. Neurologists. Tests.

The EEG showed signals in certain areas that were quieter than they should have been.

She needed speech therapy. She needed extra support in school. She learned differently than many of her classmates.

And Laniyah decided that was not going to be her story.

She wanted straight A's. If she did not understand something, she stayed after school until she did. She asked teachers to sit with her and go through it again. She would not accept a C when she believed she could do better. From grammar school through high school, every teacher said the same thing: she wants to understand. She does not want to be passed through. She works hard.

That kind of determination teaches you something as a parent.

Resilience does not always grow on an easy path. Sometimes it grows right in the middle of the challenge.

Laniyah also found soccer in fourth grade and never let it go. She ate it, slept it, breathed it. Watched footage. Studied plays. Paid for training programs on her own initiative. When opposing teams came and saw this Black American girl do everything she could do on that field, they were not always expecting it. Sometimes her coach would have her demonstrate for others.

She was operating at that level.

Her plan was to go pro. That was the whole dream. No backup. No plan B. She felt that creating a plan B meant she was already giving up on plan A — and that was not something she was willing to do.

When her school encouraged her to think about alternatives, she listened. And when asked what she would want if soccer was not an option, she finally said: I would still want to be on the field.

So she went to college for sports medicine. Not as a consolation. As a continuation. If she could not play, she would serve the ones who did.

That is Laniyah. She does not quit. She redirects.

Her senior year, she was playing a scrimmage when I got the call. I was training a client — mid-session — when my phone rang. I could hear Niyah crying loudly in the background before they even finished telling me what happened. I ended the session and got there as fast as I could. She told me she had heard a pop.

We went straight to the emergency room.

That is where we found out she had torn both her ACL and her meniscus.

Surgery followed. A long, painful recovery followed. The healing process stretched far enough that she could not finish her senior season and could not come into her first year of college playing the sport she had built her whole future around. Then, because she protected the knee out of fear and would not fully straighten it during recovery, scar tissue formed and she had to go through a second procedure to release it.

More healing. More time. More pain on top of pain.

She is fearful now of going back out on that field. And that breaks my heart — because I know this girl. I know what soccer means to her. I know she still has it in her.

I pray she finds her way back. I pray the fire returns.

She inspires me every single day. Not in an abstract way. In the specific, daily way where I look at her and think: if she can show up like that, I have no excuse.

And now, my third child.

Lavell Jr. — Mann, as we call him — came into the world fighting.

The pregnancy was intense from the beginning. He was splitting my pelvis. Complications came throughout. I was placed on bed rest. When he finally arrived, at around 36 to 37 weeks, he was not fully ready. He kept having episodes where he would stop breathing on his own. He had fluid in his stomach. He spent his first month of life in the NICU, in an incubator, with machines helping him do what his little body had not yet learned to do for itself.

I did not sleep that entire month.

And when they finally let me bring him home, I still could not sleep — because I had watched this baby stop breathing and be brought back, and now he was home, and I did not know if it would happen again.

To watch something that small fight that hard to stay in the world changes you in a way nothing else does.

He is funny, loving, and protective of his sister in a quietly tender way that gets me every time. His sense of humor — the timing, the silliness, the way he can walk into a room and shift the whole energy of it — reminds me so much of my father that sometimes it catches me off guard.

And I do not know whether to laugh or cry.

Sometimes I do both.

Niyah gave him his nickname. She had her own special way of calling him her man, her little man, hey man. And we thought it was so cute that the name just stuck.

He has been Mann ever since.

What I love about the two of them is the way they show up for each other. Even when they get on each other's nerves — which they do, because they are siblings and that is their job — the love underneath it is never in question.

When Laniyah was younger and struggled to make herself understood around people who were not used to her speech, she would say it to Mann first. And he would translate. This little

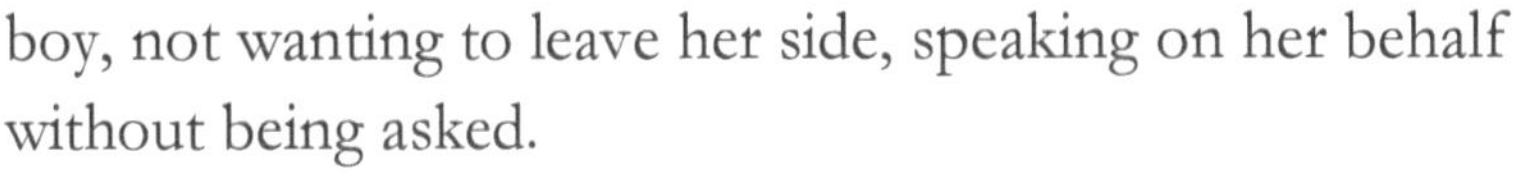

boy, not wanting to leave her side, speaking on her behalf without being asked.

I have that love on video.

I watch it more than I should.

When I left their father, I believed I was protecting my children from pain.

What I did not fully see coming was the pain that arrived anyway — just wearing a different face.

Mann told me at one point that when I divorced their dad, it felt like their father divorced them too. That without him in the household, even when his presence had been inconsistent before, at least he had been there. He would come home. He would sleep in the same space. Every now and then they would play ball together.

Once I left, even that disappeared.

I cried when he told me that.

And Mann looked at me and said: Mom, I did not tell you this to make you cry.

He pulled back after that. Started keeping things to himself to protect me from hurting. And I had to work through something hard — I had to learn how to hold their pain without falling apart in front of them. Because they needed somewhere safe to put everything down, and I wanted to be that place.

So I held my tears and held space instead. And I let them say what they needed to say.

I asked myself more than once whether I should have stayed. Whether if I had endured it longer, he would have at least been in the same household. I said it out loud to them once. I told them I was sorry. Maybe I should have stayed.

And they told me: Mom, it would not have been different. He was not really there even when he was there.

That is the thing about choices that look like sacrifices.

Sometimes what you think you are protecting people from— they are already living inside of.

We did not argue in front of the children. We did not curse each other out or call each other names in front of them. That was important to me. They heard disagreements — but not destruction. What I wanted was for them to grow up knowing that even when things fall apart, you can still choose not to burn each other down.

I hope they carry that.

There was a season when it was just the three of us — me, Laniyah, and Mann — navigating something none of us had a map for.

The separation. The new household. The uncertainty of a world that had also changed around us. Ronnie had already stepped into his own life. Their father was in his own process.

So, it was us three.

We became each other's anchor. Movie nights. New routines. Going to the gym together. Cooking together. Laughing — genuinely and often. I showed up to every event, every game, every moment that mattered. I had always been that parent. And that did not change.

What I could not do was be their father.

I never tried to pretend otherwise.

There are things a father gives his children — to his sons, to his daughter — that a mother simply cannot replicate. A son learning what it means to be a man by watching one. A daughter learning what she deserves from a man by being loved well by her first one. I could not give them that, and I knew it.

What I could give them was everything I had.

Every value. Every moral. Every dream they brought to me that I was going to support without hesitation.

Whatever you do, be the best at it.

I meant that every single time I said it.

There is something I spent years intentionally trying to break.

The pattern of passing down what we were handed without ever asking why.

There is a story about a daughter who watched her mother cut the end off a pot roast before putting it in the pan. She asked: Mom, why do you cut the end off? Her mother said: because my mother did it. So the daughter went to her grandmother and asked the same question. Grandma said: because my mother did it. So she went all the way back to her great-grandmother — Gigi — and finally got the answer:

Our pot roast pan was too small. We could not afford a bigger one, so I cut it to make it fit.

The pan had long since been replaced. The roast fit just fine now. But nobody had ever stopped to ask why — until one daughter finally did.

Generation after generation, perfectly good meat being cut off and tossed away. Not out of cruelty. Not even out of carelessness. Out of inherited habit. Out of following what was passed down without ever questioning where it came from.

That is what happens when we parent from what we were handed instead of what we have examined.

I believe my parents taught the way they were taught — passing down the patterns and teachings they had received, because that was all they knew at the time. I am not saying they were wrong. I am saying the pan had gotten bigger and no one had thought to check.

I grew up in a house where children were meant to be seen and not heard. Where having an opinion was not always welcomed.

internalized that. I spent years believing my voice did not fully belong in the room.

I decided my children would not grow up believing that.

I gave them a voice. A real one. I let them have opinions and push back respectfully. I welcomed the hard questions. I wanted them to know how to ask why — in school, in relationships, in every room they would ever walk into.

I wanted them to look at what they were handed and decide for themselves what was worth carrying and what needed to be put down.

Inside the structure of our home was always room for them to be real people.

Curious. Opinionated. Heard. Safe.

That is what I got right.

And I stand on it.

Now, I would be lying if I said the questions do not still come.

They come in the quiet. In the space between prayer and sleep when the mind goes back through the years.

Did I do enough? Could I have done more? Was I too strict? Not strict enough? Should I have shielded him more from certain influences? Should I have made different decisions along the way?

With Ronnie especially, I have turned it over more times than I can count. I never believed in keeping a child from their father unless there was real harm happening — I still believe that. But sometimes I wonder if certain exposures planted seeds I did not know were being planted.

Did I miss something I could have caught?

And then I stop myself.

Because that road — the should have, would have, could have road — has no end. You can walk it forever and never arrive anywhere useful.

With Mann, even his arrival brought questions I had no business carrying. He was a surprise. The pregnancy was complicated. And when he came out struggling, something in me went searching for fault.

That is what loving someone does — it makes you want to take responsibility for things that were never yours to carry.

But Mann is here.

Mann is whole.

Mann is Mann.

And I would not change a single thing.

The questions are part of parenting. The guilt is part of parenting. The second-guessing, the replaying — all of it comes with loving someone so completely that you feel responsible for their whole existence.

What I have had to learn, and keep relearning, is this:

You cannot parent from guilt.

At some point you have to look honestly at what you did right — really look at it — and let that stand alongside the things you would do differently.

Every parent will have moments they wish they could redo. But that does not erase the thousands of moments where you showed up, loved hard, and gave everything you had.

So, when I ask myself what I did wrong, I also remind myself of what I did right.

I loved them.

I showed up. Every game, every hospital visit, every dark season, every new beginning.

I prayed over them. Still do.

And I hugged them, told them I loved them, and made sure they grew up knowing they were protected, supported, and seen — not just as my children, but as people who mattered.

Because the story of a parent and a child does not end in one chapter. It keeps unfolding. And no matter where life takes them, one thing will always remain true.

Their mother believes in them.

Still.

Always.

Proverbs 22:6 — "Train up a child in the way he should go, and when he is old he will not depart from it."

What this means to me: I hold onto this on the hard days. Not because everything looks the way I hoped. But because I trust that what was planted does not disappear. It is working underground even when I cannot see it. The harvest is still coming.

"I did not raise perfect children. I raised real ones. And I loved them through every version of themselves they have ever been — the easy versions and the hard ones. That love has never wavered. It never will."

— *Coach Candace TW*

## For Ronnie, Laniyah, and Mann

Before the world ever had a chance
to tell you what you were worth…
I already knew.
I knew before titles.
Before mistakes.
Before choices.
Before life had a say in how you would see yourselves.
I knew.

I was still learning how to be a woman…
when they placed you in my arms.
Still trying to find my footing while teaching you how to stand.
Still searching for my voice while trying to help you find yours.
Still healing from things I didn't even have language for yet —
and somehow, in the middle of all of that…
you chose me.
And I need you to hear that part again —
You chose me.

I didn't always get it right.
There were storms I didn't know how to leave yet…
and some of that rain? It touched you too.
And for that — I'm sorry.
For every moment you felt something
that was never yours to carry…
I'm sorry.

But I need you to know this —
You were never the reason life got hard.
You were the reason I refused to stay down.
Every time life knocked me flat on my back…

it was your face that showed up in my spirit and said,
"Get up."
And I did. Every time.

I am not a perfect mother. I never was.
But I am yours.
Completely.
Not halfway. Not sometimes. Not when it's easy.
Without conditions.
Without expiration dates.
Without "if you do this, then I'll still love you."
No.
No matter what road you take.
No matter what choices you make.
No matter what chapter you're still trying to figure out —
I am still here.
And I am still yours.

So when life starts life'n — and it will —
I need you to remember this page.
Remember that a woman
who had every reason to quit…
looked at you —
and chose to keep going.
Not tomorrow. Not later.
Right then. Not today. Not ever.

So build something. Not just anything — something that lasts.
Love deeply. Not carefully — fully.
Leave something behind that speaks for you
when you're not in the room.

And understand this —
Wherever you go…
whatever room you walk into…
whatever space you step into…

you carry something nobody can take from you.
You carry where you came from.
You carry what we built.
You carry strength you didn't even realize
you were watching me practice.
You carry me.
And me?
...
I carry you.
Always.
— Mama

# CHAPTER 9

## Forgive, Don't Forget, Keep Moving

"Forgiveness is not a gift you give to the person who hurt you. It is a gift you give to yourself — so that what they did does not get to determine where you go next."

— *Coach Candace TW*

Forgiveness is one of those words people throw around like it is simple.

Just forgive. Just move on. Just let it go.

But forgiveness is rarely that neat.

Sometimes it takes time.

Sometimes it takes prayer.

Sometimes it takes distance and maturity and an understanding you simply did not have when the pain first happened.

And sometimes forgiveness does not come because someone apologized.

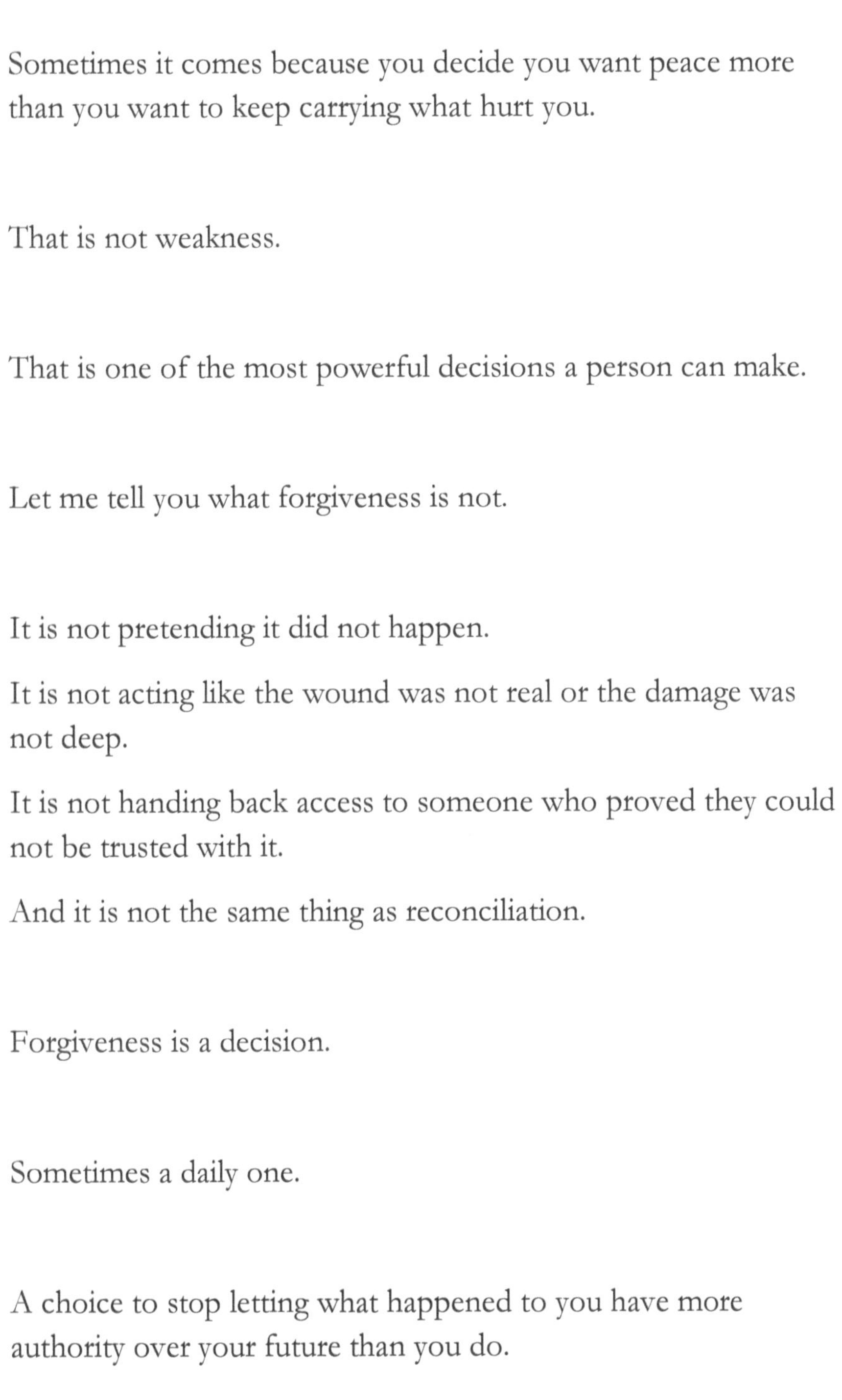

Sometimes it comes because you decide you want peace more than you want to keep carrying what hurt you.

That is not weakness.

That is one of the most powerful decisions a person can make.

Let me tell you what forgiveness is not.

It is not pretending it did not happen.

It is not acting like the wound was not real or the damage was not deep.

It is not handing back access to someone who proved they could not be trusted with it.

And it is not the same thing as reconciliation.

Forgiveness is a decision.

Sometimes a daily one.

A choice to stop letting what happened to you have more authority over your future than you do.

That distinction changed everything for me.

There is a scripture I come back to often.

Ecclesiastes 3:8 says there is a time to love and a time to hate, a time for war and a time for peace.

That scripture does not ask you to pretend every season is pleasant. It acknowledges that life has its full range — that pain and loss and betrayal are real seasons, not exceptions.

What it invites you toward is the understanding that seasons change.

That where you are right now is not where you will always be.

I have had to live that scripture out loud.

My marriage ending was one of those seasons.

After being together a little over fifteen years, what we had built together came to its close. And I want to be honest about what that felt like — because anyone who has walked through the end of a marriage knows it is not just the relationship that ends.

It is the expectations you had.

The future you imagined.

The life you thought you were building together.

The version of yourself that believed this was forever.

In those moments it is easy to become bitter.

When my husband and I separated, there was hurt. There was disappointment. There were questions about how things got to that place and what could have been done differently. I carried things in silence for a long time. I wore the mask well.

And when I finally stopped wearing it, everything I had been absorbing came flooding out in ways my body had been trying to warn me about for years.

But bitterness was not where I landed.

Instead, I found myself praying.

Not performatively. Not to look gracious.

I genuinely prayed for him. I prayed that he would heal. That he would grow into the father our children deserved. That we could find a way to co-parent from a place of health, even if that took time, even if it was messy getting there.

Some of those prayers took longer to answer than others.

But they were answered.

What we have now — the ability to be in the same room, to sit at the same table for our children, to choose peace over bitterness every time we have the opportunity to choose — that didn't happen automatically.

It was built slowly.

Through individual healing on both sides.

Through choosing again and again not to burn each other down.

There was a birthday dinner — one of those moments where life gives you a chance to see how far you have come. We were all there. Our children. People who had watched this family go through its hardest season and come out on the other side still standing. Still laughing. Still choosing each other in the ways that mattered.

I looked around that table and felt it.

Grace in the middle of chaos.

Not because everything had been perfect.

Because we had chosen something better than bitterness.

That was worth every prayer it took to get there.

Over time, something else unexpected happened.

The tension softened.

The pain did not disappear overnight, but it no longer controlled my spirit. And I realized that what I had been doing — praying for him, choosing peace, refusing to let hatred take up residence in my heart — was not just healing for us.

It was healing for me.

Because hurt people hurt people.

I believe that. I have seen it too many times not to. Understanding that did not excuse anything. But it helped me carry what I was holding without it destroying me.

Forgive. Don't forget. Keep moving.

Now I need to say something about forgiveness that most people are never told.

Saying the words is not the same thing as doing the work.

I have watched people say I forgive you and mean it — genuinely mean it in that moment — and still carry every ounce of the wound for years afterward.

Not because they were lying.

Because forgiveness is not a declaration.

It is a process.

And the process takes longer than the words.

Here is how you know the process is not finished yet.

When you bring up what happened —

and your body responds the same way it did when it first happened.

The chest tightening.

The anger rising.

The image replaying.

The emotion flooding back.

That is not forgiveness taking hold.

That is stored pain still firing.

Your nervous system does not know the difference between a memory and a present threat.

When the wound is unresolved, the brain replays it —

and the body relives it.

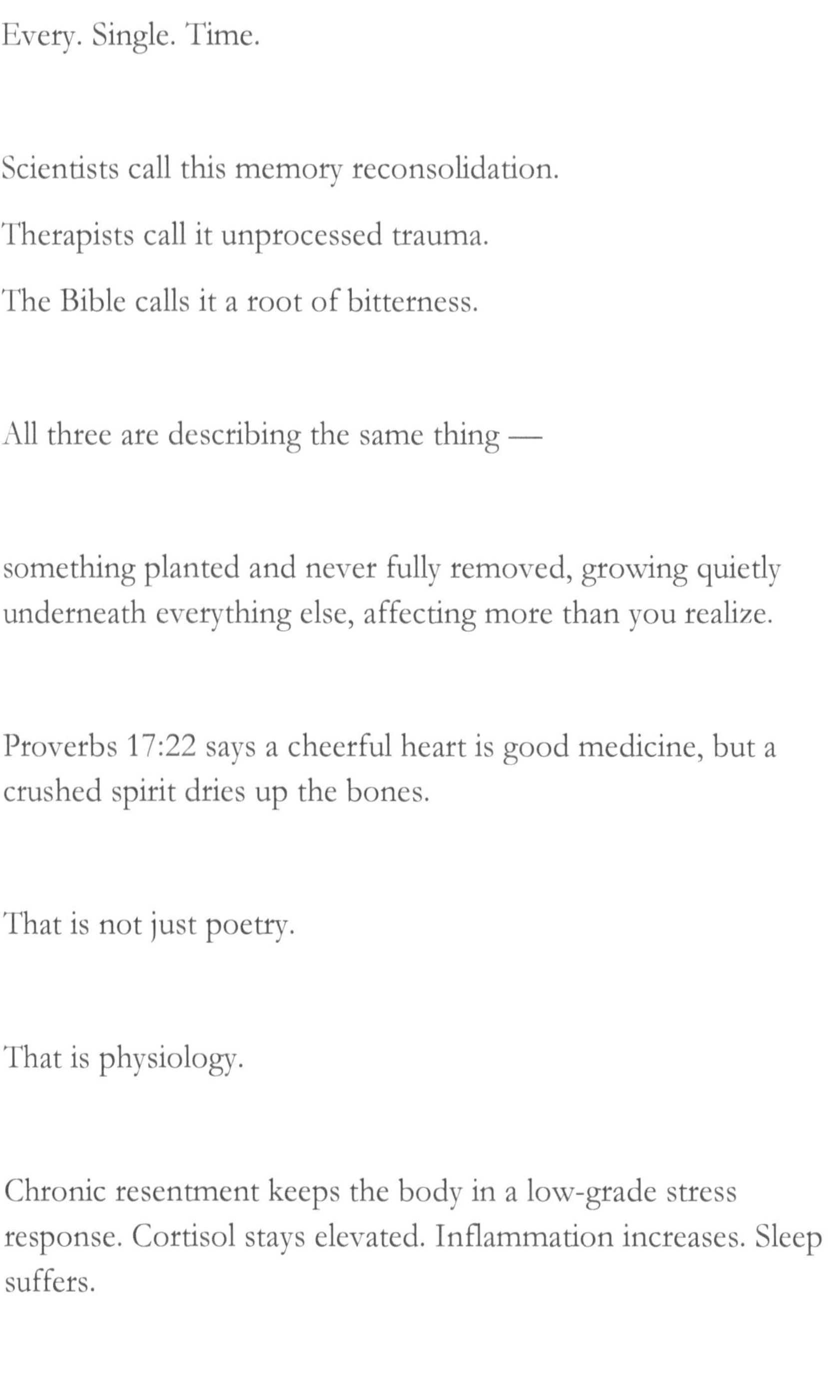

Every. Single. Time.

Scientists call this memory reconsolidation.

Therapists call it unprocessed trauma.

The Bible calls it a root of bitterness.

All three are describing the same thing —

something planted and never fully removed, growing quietly underneath everything else, affecting more than you realize.

Proverbs 17:22 says a cheerful heart is good medicine, but a crushed spirit dries up the bones.

That is not just poetry.

That is physiology.

Chronic resentment keeps the body in a low-grade stress response. Cortisol stays elevated. Inflammation increases. Sleep suffers.

The person who hurt you may have moved on completely —

and your body is still paying the price of carrying what happened.

Hebrews 12:15 warns about a bitter root that grows up and causes trouble.

It spreads.

It defiles.

Not just the relationship with the person who hurt you — but everything the bitterness touches.

Your peace.

Your health.

Your ability to receive what is good because part of you is still braced for harm.

And Philippians 4:8 tells us to think on what is true, noble, right, pure, lovely, and admirable.

Why?

Because what we rehearse in our minds grows stronger in our lives.

What you keep replaying, you keep feeding.

And what you keep feeding eventually controls how you see everything around you.

Real forgiveness looks different from performed forgiveness.

Real forgiveness is when you can tell the story without reliving it.

When the image does not replay.

When the anger does not rise.

When you can speak about what happened from a place of peace instead of pain —

not because you forgot,

not because it did not matter,

but because you are no longer living inside it.

I know the moment it happened for me.

I was talking about one of the hardest things I had ever carried — something I had told before through tears and through anger — and something was different.

The image did not come.

The feeling did not flood back.

I was present.

I was clear.

I could speak the truth of what happened without my body treating it like it was happening right now.

That was not the absence of memory.

That was the presence of healing.

And I want you to hear this clearly —

especially if you have been telling yourself you have forgiven someone while still replaying every detail of what they did, still measuring their current behavior against what they owe you, still feeling the sting rise every time their name comes up:

You have not forgiven yet.

And that is okay.

It does not make you a bad person.

It does not mean you are weak.

It means you are human and the wound was real and the healing is still in progress.

But do not call it finished when it is not.

Because forgiveness that is not yet complete cannot be rushed by pretending. It has to be walked through. Prayed through. Processed through.

Sometimes with a therapist.

Sometimes on your knees.

Sometimes through the slow, daily decision to stop rehearsing the pain and start releasing it.

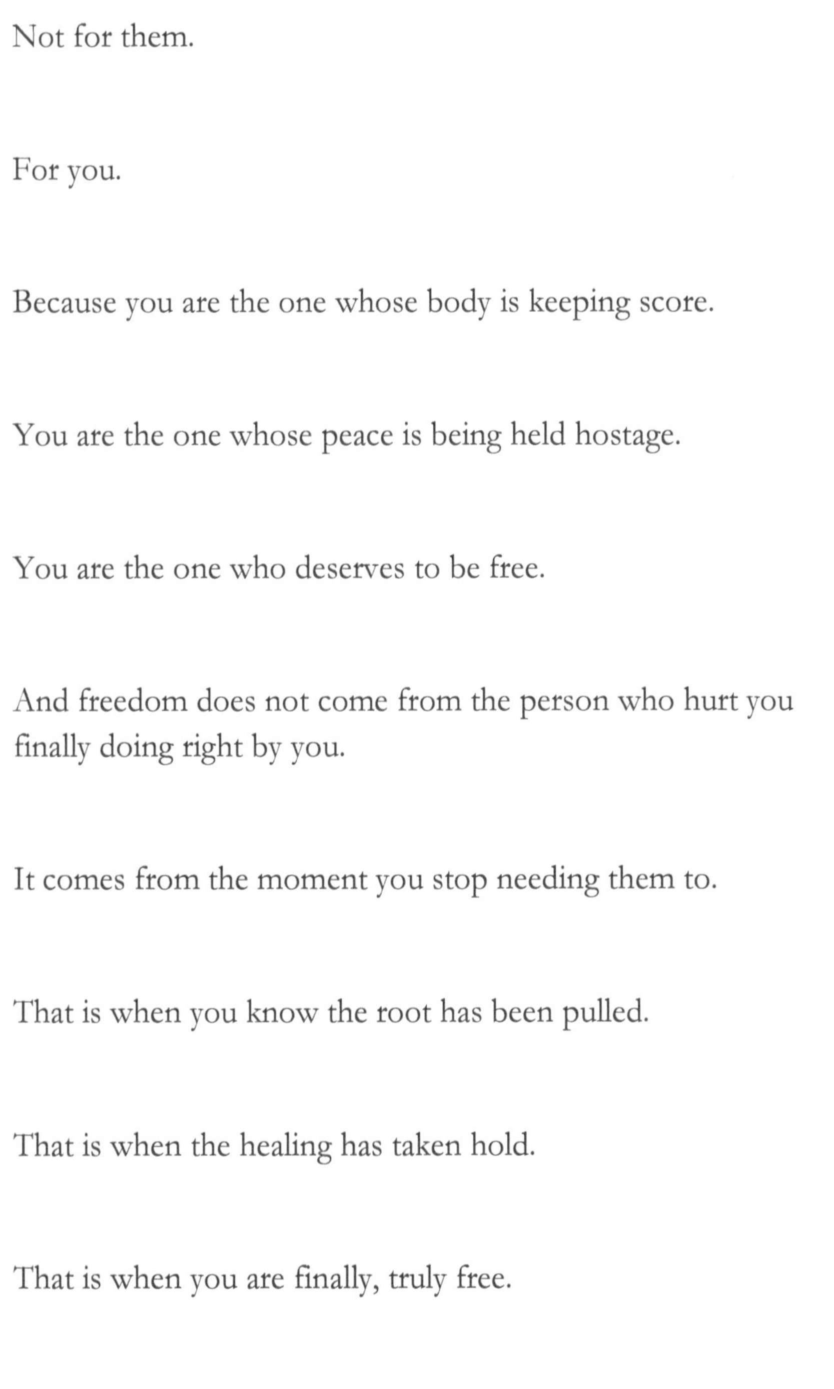

Not for them.

For you.

Because you are the one whose body is keeping score.

You are the one whose peace is being held hostage.

You are the one who deserves to be free.

And freedom does not come from the person who hurt you finally doing right by you.

It comes from the moment you stop needing them to.

That is when you know the root has been pulled.

That is when the healing has taken hold.

That is when you are finally, truly free.

Now let me say something that needs to be said clearly.

There is a difference between forgiveness and reconciliation that most people never get taught.

Reconciliation requires accountability, change, and consistency

—

from both sides.

Forgiveness requires only one person.

You.

That is why you can forgive someone and still move on without them.

Forgiveness is about your heart.

Not their behavior.

And some people will never apologize — not because they forgot what they did, but because taking accountability would require more of them than they are ready to give.

If your healing depends on their apology —

you will stay stuck.

So you forgive anyway.

Not because they earned it.

But because you are not carrying it anymore.

Forgiveness says: I release you.

Wisdom says: I don't stand there anymore.

Both are required.

Forgiving someone does not mean keeping them close.

Forgiveness and access are not the same thing.

You can fully release someone from the debt of what they owe you without ever giving them back the proximity they had before.

Some people get forgiven from a distance.

Some relationships get released, not repaired.

That is not a failure of grace.

That is wisdom.

Forgiveness also required me to look at my family with a deeper level of understanding.

When you grow up, you start to see your parents differently. As a child you see them as the authority — the ones who should have known everything, gotten everything right.

But adulthood teaches you something humbling.

Your parents were learning too.

They were navigating life with the tools they had. The experiences they came from. The upbringing they knew. And just like the pot roast story from the last chapter — sometimes people pass down what they were given without ever stopping to ask if the pan had gotten bigger.

That does not mean every decision was perfect. Some things could have been handled differently. Some moments needed more support or more understanding than they received.

But as I grew older, I began to see the bigger picture.

I could see where they came from.

I could see the pressures they carried.

I could see the ways they loved, even when it was not always expressed in the way I needed at the time.

And understanding that made forgiveness possible.

Not because everything was fine.

Because they were human.

And just like I hope my children will one day give me grace for the seasons I navigated imperfectly, I had to learn how to give that same grace to the people who raised me.

That does not erase the past.

It simply allows your heart to soften toward it.

One of the more complicated layers of forgiveness involved something deeply personal from earlier in my life.

I talked about it in Chapter 4 — the things that happened to me when I was young, and the ways people around me responded when they found out.

My mother loved me.

I have never doubted that.

But in the moment I needed her most, something in her went quiet. The embarrassment, the shock, the weight of not knowing how to respond — it all got bigger than the space I needed from her.

For a long time, I carried questions about that.

As I matured, I began to see something I could not see from inside the pain.

My mother carried it too.

She carried guilt.

She carried regret.

She carried the weight of wishing she could go back and respond differently.

Forgiveness does not always mean someone meant to hurt you. Sometimes it means recognizing that people react out of shock, out of their own wounds, out of limitations they did not even know they had.

Sometimes the person who needed to be held was standing next to someone who did not know how to hold them —

not because they did not love them,

but because they had never been taught how.

I do not want my mother carrying that guilt for the rest of her life.

She gave me her blessing to tell this story.

She said: it is yours to tell.

And so I tell it — not to wound her, but to free us both.

Mom, I forgive you. Fully. I love you. And it is time to put it down.

Forgiveness has been necessary in other relationships too.

Moments of betrayal.

Moments when people showed sides of themselves I did not expect.

Moments when trust was broken in ways I had to decide whether to repair or release.

But forgiveness does not mean pretending those things did not happen.

It means I refuse to let those experiences harden my heart.

Because when you carry unforgiveness long enough, it does not just affect your relationship with the person who hurt you —

it affects your peace,

your outlook,

your ability to trust again.

It lives in your body and creates the very dis-ease that, held long enough, becomes disease.

Forgiveness is not just a spiritual principle.

It is a health decision.

So I forgave. But I kept the lessons.

The lessons taught me how to set better boundaries. How to recognize the signs sooner. How to protect what is mine — my peace, my energy, my access — before it is taken rather than after.

There is a poem most people know — Footprints in the Sand, written by Margaret Fishback Powers in 1964.

Two sets of footprints moving through life — and then through the hardest seasons, only one.

The person asks God: where were you when I needed you most?

And the answer is: those are the seasons I was carrying you.

I have thought about that more times than I can count.

Because when I look back at the seasons when everything was stripped — when the hurt was deepest, the path was darkest, the options felt the smallest —

I can see it now.

The person who showed up at exactly the right moment.

The door that opened just in time.

The prayer that got answered in a form I did not recognize until later.

He was carrying me.

Not in spite of the hard seasons.

Through them. Inside them.

And I was not alone.

Even when it felt that way.

Even when nobody knew.

Even when I was the one holding everybody else up with a smile on my face.

He was there.

Two things I know for sure:

Prayers work.

And tables eventually turn.

I have watched it happen. I have lived it happen. I have been in seasons where everything looked impossible, where the odds were stacked and the only thing left was faith and the words I was still speaking over my own life —

and then watched the table turn in ways I could not have engineered on my own.

I am not asking you to believe everything I believe.

I am asking you to look at your own life.

Look at the seasons you thought would finish you.

Look at where you are standing right now.

The table turned.

Maybe slowly.

Maybe not in the way you expected.

Maybe the turning looked different than the version you had been holding in your prayers.

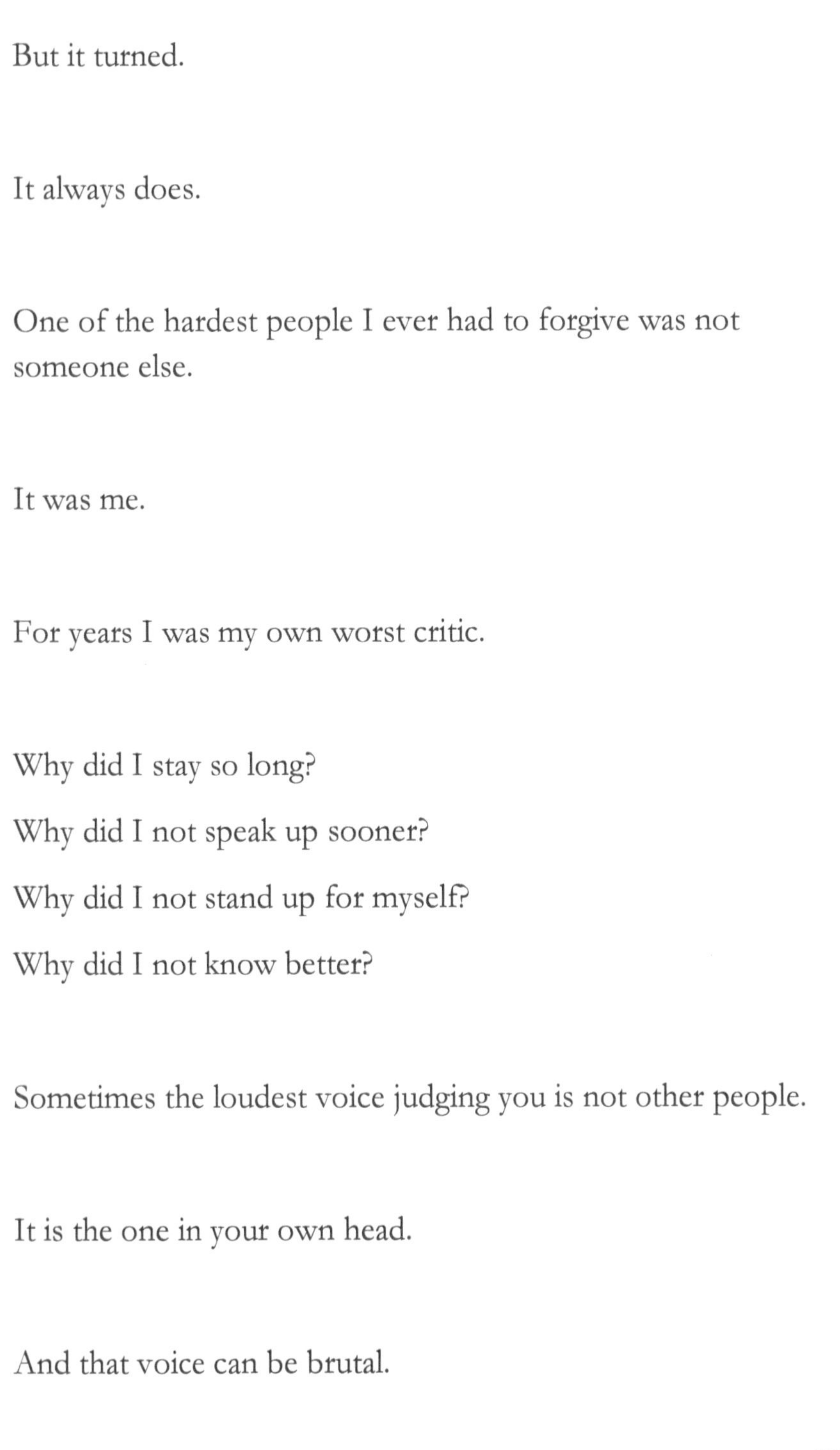

But it turned.

It always does.

One of the hardest people I ever had to forgive was not someone else.

It was me.

For years I was my own worst critic.

Why did I stay so long?

Why did I not speak up sooner?

Why did I not stand up for myself?

Why did I not know better?

Sometimes the loudest voice judging you is not other people.

It is the one in your own head.

And that voice can be brutal.

I had to learn that forgiveness is not only something we extend to others.

Sometimes the person who needs it most is the one staring back at you in the mirror.

Because the truth is this:

You cannot punish your younger self for not having the knowledge your older self has now.

That younger version of you was still learning.

Still growing.

Still trying to survive and make sense of life with the tools available at the time.

The same grace we extend to others is the grace we must learn to give ourselves.

I forgive the younger version of me who did not know what I know now.

I forgive the girl who carried shame and blamed herself for what was done to her.

I forgive the young mother who was figuring life out while raising a life at the same time.

I forgive the woman who stayed in places that drained her while she was still learning her worth.

I forgive the version of me that got so tired, so overwhelmed, she questioned if she even wanted to keep going.

I forgive her too.

Those seasons did not destroy you.

They shaped you.

They molded you.

They built the version of you standing here right now.

There is another layer of forgiveness I had to face that many people never talk about.

The shame we carry about our own story.

For a long time, I carried embarrassment that did not even belong to me.

Embarrassed about becoming a young mother.

Embarrassed about things that happened to me when I was young that were never my fault.

Embarrassed that I did not have everything figured out sooner.

Embarrassed that my life did not look the way I thought it would by a certain point.

And when you carry that kind of embarrassment long enough, it quietly becomes something heavier.

Shame.

But healing requires a moment where you stop and ask yourself honestly:

Why am I carrying shame for things that helped shape the woman I am today?

That younger version of me was not weak.

She was surviving.

That young mother was not a failure.

She was doing the best she could with the tools she had.

That young woman who stayed quiet about certain things was not broken.

She was trying to understand something she had never been prepared to face.

And once I saw it that way, something shifted.

That girl and that young woman did not deserve my judgment.

They deserved compassion.

They deserved understanding.

They deserved grace.

So, I forgave her too.

I forgave the younger version of myself who was still learning life. Because if I keep punishing her for not being perfect, I will never fully appreciate the strength it took for her to become the woman I am today.

Every chapter of our lives — even the messy ones — becomes part of the foundation that builds who we are still becoming.

So I released the shame.

I kept the lessons.

And I kept moving.

A Declaration of Grace

Today I release the weight of the past.

I forgive the people who hurt me.

I forgive the people who disappointed me.

And most importantly, I forgive myself.

I forgive the younger version of me who did not know what I know now.

I forgive the girl who stayed silent because she was scared.

I forgive the young mother who was figuring out life while raising children at the same time.

I forgive the woman who stayed in places longer than she should have because she was still learning her worth.

I will no longer punish myself for surviving seasons I had never been taught how to navigate.

I will no longer carry shame for things that helped shape the strength I walk in today.

I keep the lessons.

I keep the wisdom.

But I release the weight.

I release the embarrassment.

I release the guilt.

I release the voice that says I should have been perfect.

Because perfection was never the assignment.

Growth was.

So today I choose grace.

Grace for the girl I used to be.

Grace for the woman I am still becoming.

I forgive.

I don't forget the lessons.

And I keep moving.

Repeat this to yourself:

What was done to me does not define me.

I release what I was never meant to carry.

I forgive — not for them, but for me.

I keep moving.

Before you leave this chapter:

Think about one thing you have been holding — something you told yourself you released but that still surfaces when you are quiet. Name it honestly. Not to punish yourself for still carrying it. Just to see it clearly.

Then ask yourself: what would it feel like to set this down? Not to forget it happened. Not to pretend it did not matter. Just to stop giving it weight in your future.

That is where forgiveness begins. Not in a dramatic moment. In a quiet decision to stop letting the past be the loudest voice in the room.

Ecclesiastes 3:8 — "A time to love and a time to hate, a time for war and a time for peace."

What this means to me: Every season has its purpose. Even the painful ones. Even the ones that did not make sense while you were living inside them. The goal is not to rush through the hard seasons pretending they are not real. The goal is to move through them without letting them become permanent addresses.

Matthew 6:14 — "For if you forgive other people when they sin against you, your heavenly Father will also forgive you."

What this means to me: Forgiveness is not about excusing what happened. It is about releasing what is no longer mine to carry.

When I forgive, I am not letting anyone off the hook with God. I am freeing myself from the hook that unforgiveness had in me. I trust God with the rest.

"Forgive, don't forget, and keep moving. Not because what happened did not matter. Because you do."

— *Coach Candace TW*

"I forgave you not because you deserved it, but because I deserved peace. And I chose myself enough to move forward without carrying what tried to break me."

— *Coach Candace TW*

# Fifty Shades of Forgiveness

Forgiveness don't always
come in one color.
Sometimes it's soft —
the kind you give
to someone who loved you
the best way they knew how
even when the best way
wasn't enough.
Sometimes it's quiet —
the kind that never gets spoken out loud
but lives in the way
you still answer the phone.
Still show up.
Still choose love
over the version of the story
that would let you walk away clean.
And sometimes —
sometimes forgiveness is hard.
The kind you have to wrestle out of yourself
on your knees
at two in the morning
when the wound is still fresh
and everything in you
wants to hold onto it
just a little longer.

But I let it go.
Not because it didn't matter.
Because I matter more.

There are people in my story
who will read these words

and know.
They will not need me
to say their name.
They will feel it
the way you feel a room
go quiet when you walk in —
that particular silence
that tells you
the conversation
was just about you.

To the one who stayed silent
when silence was the last thing I needed —
I understand now
what shame looks like
when it wears love's face.
I understand now
that some people are standing
in the middle of their own storm
when yours hits —
and they reach for you
and miss
not because they don't care
but because
they cannot see past
their own rain.
I forgive you.
Not with conditions.
Not with footnotes.
Just —
I forgive you.
Put it down.
We are not living there anymore.

To the ones
who took without asking —

who mistook my softness
for an open door,
my patience
for permission,
my grace
for weakness —
I want you to sit with something.
Everything you tried to take from me —
the peace,
the power,
the parts of me
that were never yours —
I still have it.
All of it.
You cannot steal
what God sealed
inside a woman
before she even knew
she was carrying it.

But I let it go.
Not because it didn't matter.
Because I matter more.

To the ones who built fires
and handed me the blame —
to the ones who lied
so smoothly
even they believed it —
to the ones who saw my light
and tried to live in it
without ever learning
how to tend it —
I am not angry anymore.
Angry is a weight
I stopped paying rent on

a long time ago.
What I feel now
is something quieter.
Something that sounds like:
I see you.
I see what you were carrying
when you did what you did.
I see the wound inside the wound.
And I release you from mine.

Because here is what I learned
about forgiveness —
it is not a feeling.
It is a decision.
Made sometimes daily.
Sometimes hourly.
Sometimes in the middle of a memory
that shows up uninvited
and sits down at your table
like it owns the place.
And you look at it.
You name it.
You say —
I see you.
And I am not carrying you anymore.

But I let it go.
Not because it didn't matter.
Because I matter more.

Some of you will read this
and feel relieved.
Some of you will read this
and feel the sting
of being forgiven
by someone

who had every right
to never speak your name again —
and chose grace anyway.
Let that land.
Let it do what it came to do.
Not to shame you.
To free you.
Because here is the truth
nobody tells you
about being forgiven —
it is a gift
you did not earn.
And the woman giving it
does not need a single thing
from you in return.
Not an apology.
Not an explanation.
Not the confession
that she was the one
holding everything together
while you were coming undone.
She already knew.
She just decided
that your debt
was no longer her burden to hold —
and traded the weight of it
for something worth more
than being owed.

This is…

Fifty shades of forgiveness.
Every color.
Every shade.
Every layered,
complicated,

necessary piece of it —
until the last shade fell away
and what was left
had a name.
Free.

Not because it was easy.
Because I was worth
every shade
it took
to get here.

I forgave.
I kept the lessons.
I dropped the weight.
And I walked out of every version of that pain
into the light —
unbothered,
unbroken,
and finally,
finally —
fifty shades freed.

# CHAPTER 10

## Still Standing

"Strength is not about never falling. It is about who you become every time you rise."

— *Coach Candace TW*

For a long time, I thought I had to wait.

Wait until my life was completely put together.

Wait until the pain had been fully resolved, the lessons completely learned, the success fully achieved.

Wait until I could look back at everything and say —

now it makes sense. Now I am ready. Now I can tell the story.

I thought by the time I finished writing this book, I needed to have it all figured out.

The perfect life.

The perfect peace.

The perfect ending.

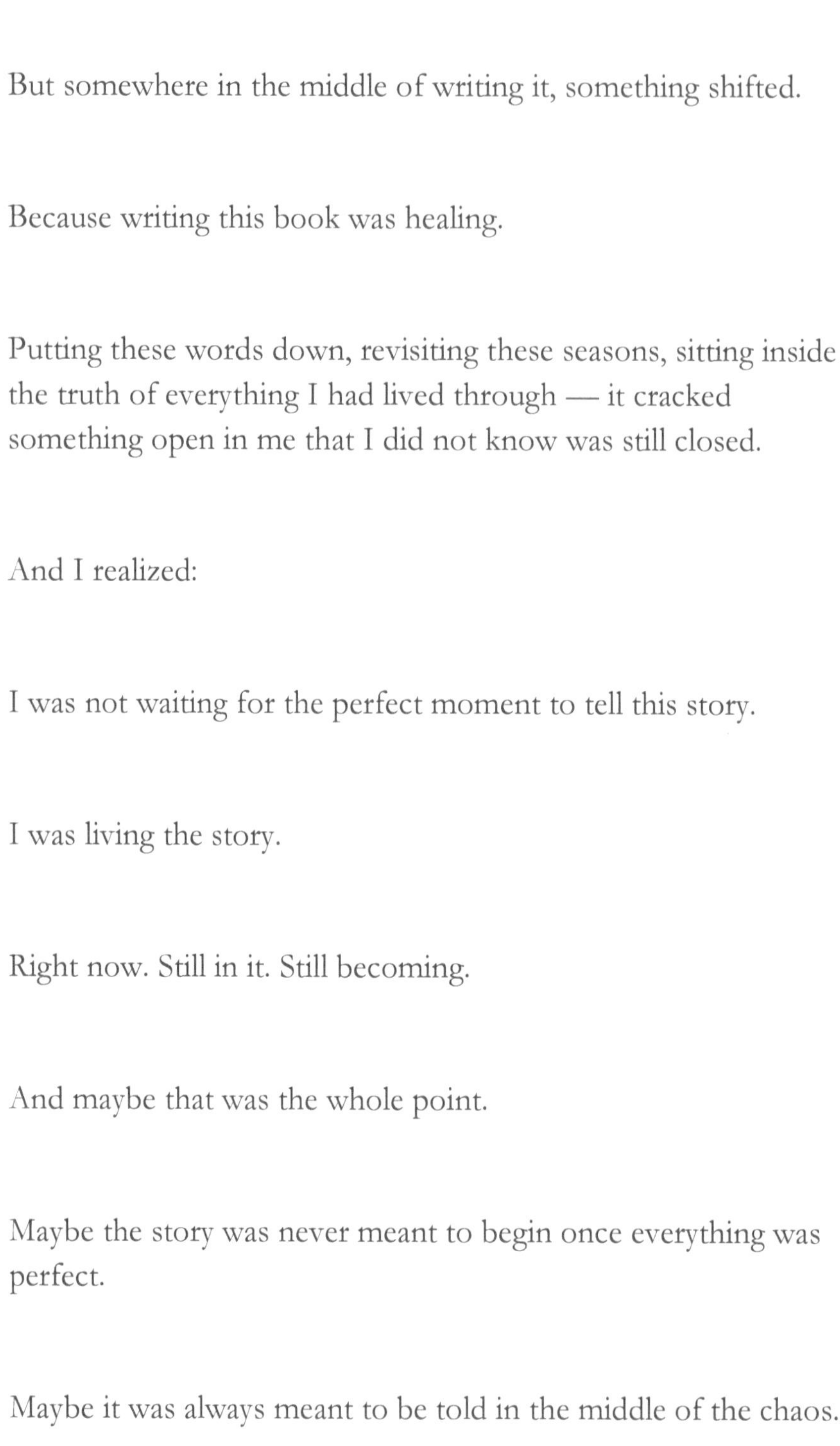

But somewhere in the middle of writing it, something shifted.

Because writing this book was healing.

Putting these words down, revisiting these seasons, sitting inside the truth of everything I had lived through — it cracked something open in me that I did not know was still closed.

And I realized:

I was not waiting for the perfect moment to tell this story.

I was living the story.

Right now. Still in it. Still becoming.

And maybe that was the whole point.

Maybe the story was never meant to begin once everything was perfect.

Maybe it was always meant to be told in the middle of the chaos.

Because that is where grace lives.

Grace does not show up when everything is easy. Grace shows up when life feels uncertain and you choose to keep moving anyway. Grace shows up in the middle of the mess, in the middle of the rebuilding, in the middle of the not-yet —

and it holds you there until the next chapter begins.

Grace in the middle of chaos.

That is this book. That is this life.

There is something about surviving your own story that nobody prepares you for.

Not the surviving itself.

The standing on the other side of it.

Looking back at everything you came through and realizing — somehow, through all of it —

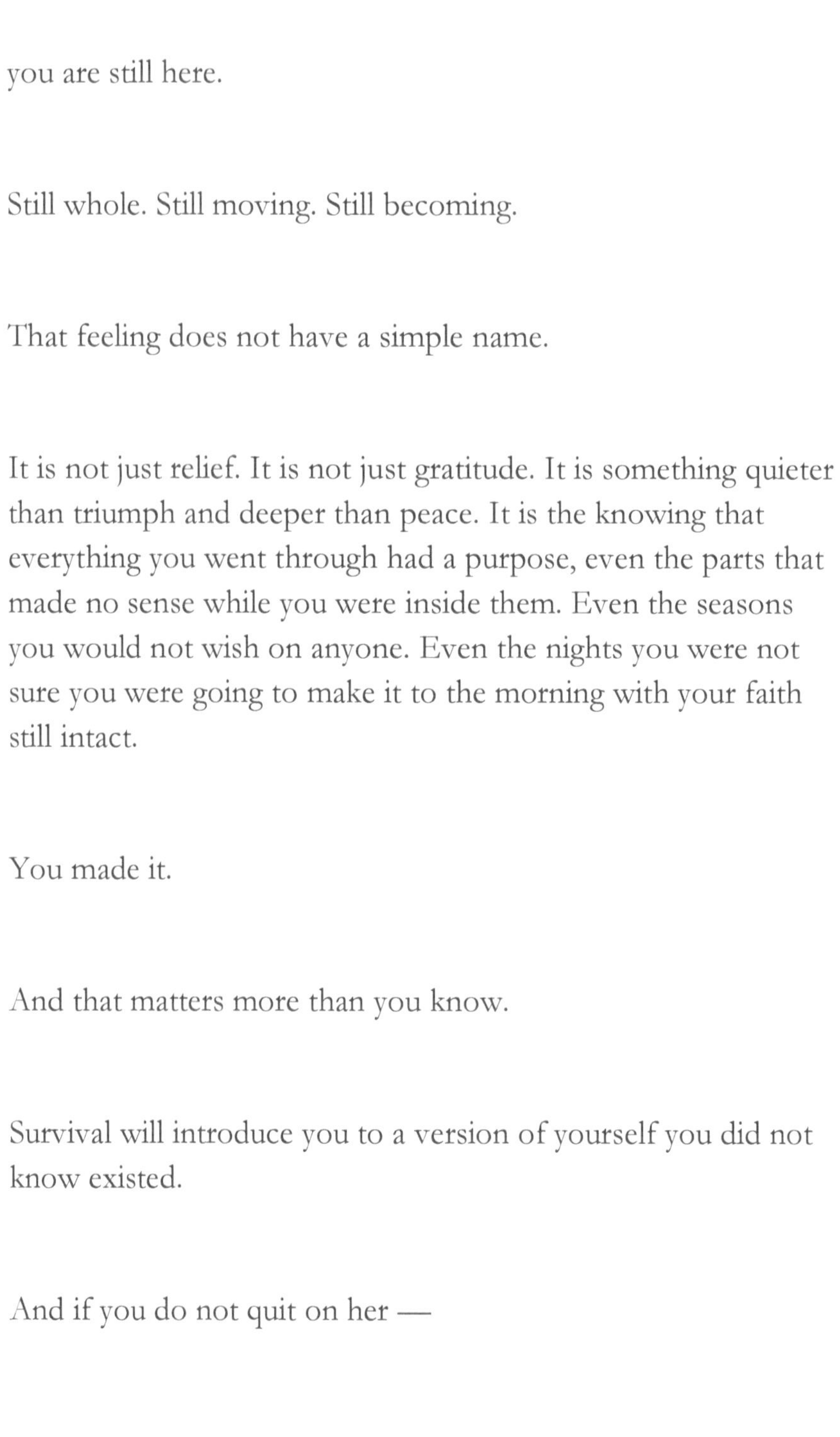

you are still here.

Still whole. Still moving. Still becoming.

That feeling does not have a simple name.

It is not just relief. It is not just gratitude. It is something quieter than triumph and deeper than peace. It is the knowing that everything you went through had a purpose, even the parts that made no sense while you were inside them. Even the seasons you would not wish on anyone. Even the nights you were not sure you were going to make it to the morning with your faith still intact.

You made it.

And that matters more than you know.

Survival will introduce you to a version of yourself you did not know existed.

And if you do not quit on her —

she will turn into someone powerful.

I think about where I started.

Not just the beginning of this book — the beginning of me.

The girl who had it all planned out before life reached in and rearranged everything. The girl who still believed, even in the dark, that if she said something and meant it, it would happen. The girl who kept writing poems until someone took that too.

She did not know then what I know now.

She did not know that every single thing she was walking through was building something. That the weight was not punishment — it was preparation. That the breaking was not the end of her —

it was the beginning of who she was becoming.

There is a reason Maya Angelou wrote Still I Rise. Because that is what women who have been through the fire do.

They rise.

Not in spite of what tried to break them.

Because of what it built in them.

That poem was written for every woman who was counted out, pushed down, silenced, or underestimated — and got up anyway.

I felt that poem in my bones long before I fully understood my own story.

If I could go back and sit with that younger version of me for a moment, I would not tell her it was going to be easy.

I would tell her: keep going. It is worth it. You are worth it. And one day you are going to look back at all of this and understand exactly why.

There were moments when I questioned everything.

Moments when I wondered if I had made too many wrong choices.

Moments when I thought I should have been further along by now.

Moments when the dreams I was carrying felt too big for the life I was currently living.

But every time I got close to giving up, something inside me said the same thing.

Keep going.

Not because the path was clear.

Not because the outcome was guaranteed.

But because stopping would mean giving up on the life that was still unfolding in front of me.

And I had not come through everything I had come through to stop here.

The comeback is always louder than the setback — if you don't quit on yourself.

So, I kept going.

I kept planting seeds when I could not see the harvest.

I kept speaking life when the circumstances were not cooperating.

I kept showing up for other people even in the seasons when I was barely showing up for myself —

because somewhere in me I understood that what I was building was bigger than any single difficult season.

I talked in an earlier chapter about the woman who approached me at a bodybuilding competition. The one who said: because of you, I did this. I think about that moment often — because I had been planting seeds into what sometimes felt like silence, posting to four people, wondering if any of it mattered. And there she was, telling me it had grown into something she carried into her hardest moments.

That moment motivated me more than I had motivated her that day.

Because it reminded me that even in the seasons when I was exhausted, even when I was in the dark behind the smile —

the seeds were still growing in places I could not see.

Keep planting. Even when you cannot see the harvest. Especially then.

Everyone you admire has failed.

Every person who built something meaningful has had seasons where the outcome looked uncertain. Where the doubt was louder than the dream. Where starting over felt like losing when it was actually redirecting.

The difference between them and the people who never got there is not talent.

It is not luck.

It is not a better starting point.

It is that they kept going.

They tried again. They adjusted. They stayed in the room when everything in them wanted to leave. They made the decision, again and again, to keep moving forward even when forward did not look the way they expected.

Growth is rarely dramatic.

It is usually built through small, consistent decisions that do not look like much in the moment but compound into something undeniable over time.

Nobody watches you harder than the people who doubted you.

Give them a good show.

Not out of spite — out of purpose.

A life lived fully, a dream pursued relentlessly, a woman standing in everything she survived and still moving forward —

that is worth watching.

And more than that —

it is worth living.

I want to say something about building — about the kind of building that outlasts you.

This is something I am still in the middle of learning, still in the process of applying to my own life. And I am not going to pretend otherwise.

But I am learning it because I understand something I did not always understand:

Wealth is not just about money.

It is about knowledge.

It is about changing the conversation your family has about money.

It is about being the person who finally understands the difference between what builds you up and what quietly drains you.

About creating multiple ways to sustain yourself so that when one door slows down, you are not starting from nothing.

I grew up watching people work hard and still come up short — not because they did not try, but because the knowledge was not in the room. Nobody taught them.

So I decided to start learning.

Started asking questions.

Started studying what I did not know so that one day I could pass down something different.

If nobody in your home growing up ever talked about this — let me say it now.

You deserve to build.

You deserve to understand how to make your money work. You deserve to leave something behind that outlasts you.

Start where you are. Start with what you have.

But start.

The table you set today is the one your children and their children will eat from.

I want to talk about energy for a moment.

Not in a way that is hard to grasp — in the most practical, human way I know how to describe it.

I have watched science and faith meet each other in places people do not expect. There is research on the electromagnetic field the human body produces. On how the frequency you carry — your thoughts, your emotional state, the way you walk into a room — radiates outward and interacts with the world around you whether you are aware of it or not.

I believe that.

Because I have lived it.

Even in my darkest seasons — the ones I have shared in this book and the ones I never spoke publicly — people told me they felt something when they were around me. That I was their peace. That something about my presence made them feel safe enough to open up. That hearing my voice made them feel like they could exhale.

That was not because my life was perfect.

It was not because I had it all together.

It was because the frequency I chose to operate at — the genuine one, the one rooted in faith and love and the decision to keep showing up — that radiated outward even when I was hurting on the inside.

Be the energy you seek.

If you want peace, be peace.

If you want genuine love, be genuine love.

If you want to be surrounded by people who are growing, be someone who is growing.

You do not attract what you want.

You attract what you are.

Do the work on the inside.

Because the inside is what broadcasts.

I need to tell you about a day that changed something in me.

I ran into a grocery store to use the restroom. Since I was already there, I decided to check if they had my favorite vegan cupcakes. As I was heading toward the bakery, a man approached me.

He asked about the ingredients on a bottle of freshly squeezed orange juice he was holding. I answered. We exchanged a few words. I kept walking toward the bakery.

They were sold out.

I turned to leave.

And he stopped me again.

He started asking me about a gift of mine.

Something in me slowed down.

Because this total stranger began to speak things over my life that no one should have known. He talked about my children. Their personalities. Their paths. Specific enough that I stood there unable to move.

He told me about my light.

He said that what I had survived, most people would not have survived. That they would have broken. That the things I had walked through in silence would have put other people in a straitjacket.

He said I was a healer.

He kept talking. And I kept listening. Because everything he said was landing.

Not in a general way.

In a how do you know that way.

I thought I would be in and out of that store in ten minutes.

I looked up and almost two hours had passed.

Eventually I said — well, since I am here, let me grab some water. We walked together. He still had that one little juice carton. When we got to the register, I looked at him and said: are you going to get something?

He said: no. I came here for you.

He helped me carry my water to the car. Grabbed two jugs and told me I could carry the rest because I was strong. We laughed. I asked for his name and his number. He gave them to me. I called the number right then. His phone rang.

He said goodbye. I got in the car.

I looked down to start the engine.

I looked back up.

He was gone.

Not walking away. Not turning a corner.

Gone.

There was not enough time. He was an older man. There was nowhere he could have disappeared to that fast.

I told my mom. She listened to the whole story and did not hesitate.

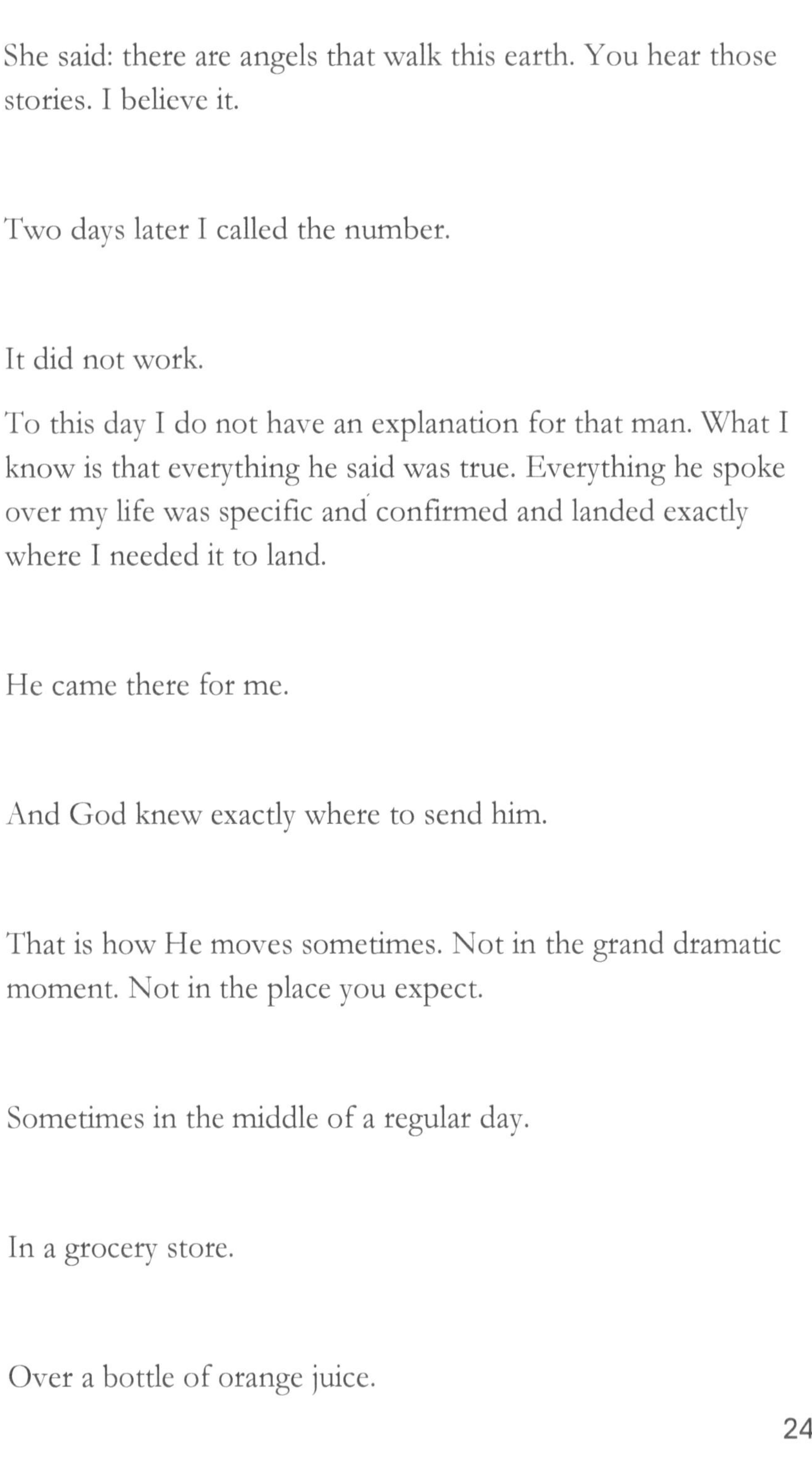

She said: there are angels that walk this earth. You hear those stories. I believe it.

Two days later I called the number.

It did not work.

To this day I do not have an explanation for that man. What I know is that everything he said was true. Everything he spoke over my life was specific and confirmed and landed exactly where I needed it to land.

He came there for me.

And God knew exactly where to send him.

That is how He moves sometimes. Not in the grand dramatic moment. Not in the place you expect.

Sometimes in the middle of a regular day.

In a grocery store.

Over a bottle of orange juice.

He always knows where to find you.

Life be life'n.

I have said that since the beginning of this book and I meant it every time.

Life does not pause. It does not wait for convenient timing. Bills come when they come. Hearts break when they break. Plans fall apart when they fall apart.

Life be life'n.

But here is what I also know — what I have built my life on, what I have watched prove itself true again and again in ways I could not have engineered on my own:

God still God'n.

He was in the room when two women knocked on my door in December with a letter I had forgotten I wrote.

He was in every prayer that felt like it was going nowhere until it arrived everywhere at once.

He was in the healing that came slowly and then suddenly.

He was in the table that turned when I had stopped watching for it to turn.

He was carrying me through the seasons I could not carry myself — and some of those seasons, I did not even realize I was being carried until I looked back and saw only one set of footprints.

That is not a performance of faith.

That is testimony.

And a testimony does not stay quiet. It finds its way out. It finds the person who needs it. It becomes the reason someone else decides to keep going on a day they were ready to stop.

That is why I wrote this book.

Not because I have arrived.

Not because everything I have been believing for has already shown up in the forms I imagined.

Not because my life is the finished version.

But because I am still here.

Still building.

Still praying.

Still speaking life over what has not yet come.

Still choosing faith over fear, even on the mornings when fear is louder.

And I wanted you to see that.

The real version. With all the chapters included. Not just the ones that looked good.

When I look back over everything I have lived through, I no longer see only the pain.

I see the transformation.

I see the young girl who carried shame that was never hers growing into a woman who put it down and refused to pick it back up.

I see the young mother who was figuring out life while raising a child growing into someone who learned to forgive herself for not knowing what she had not yet been taught.

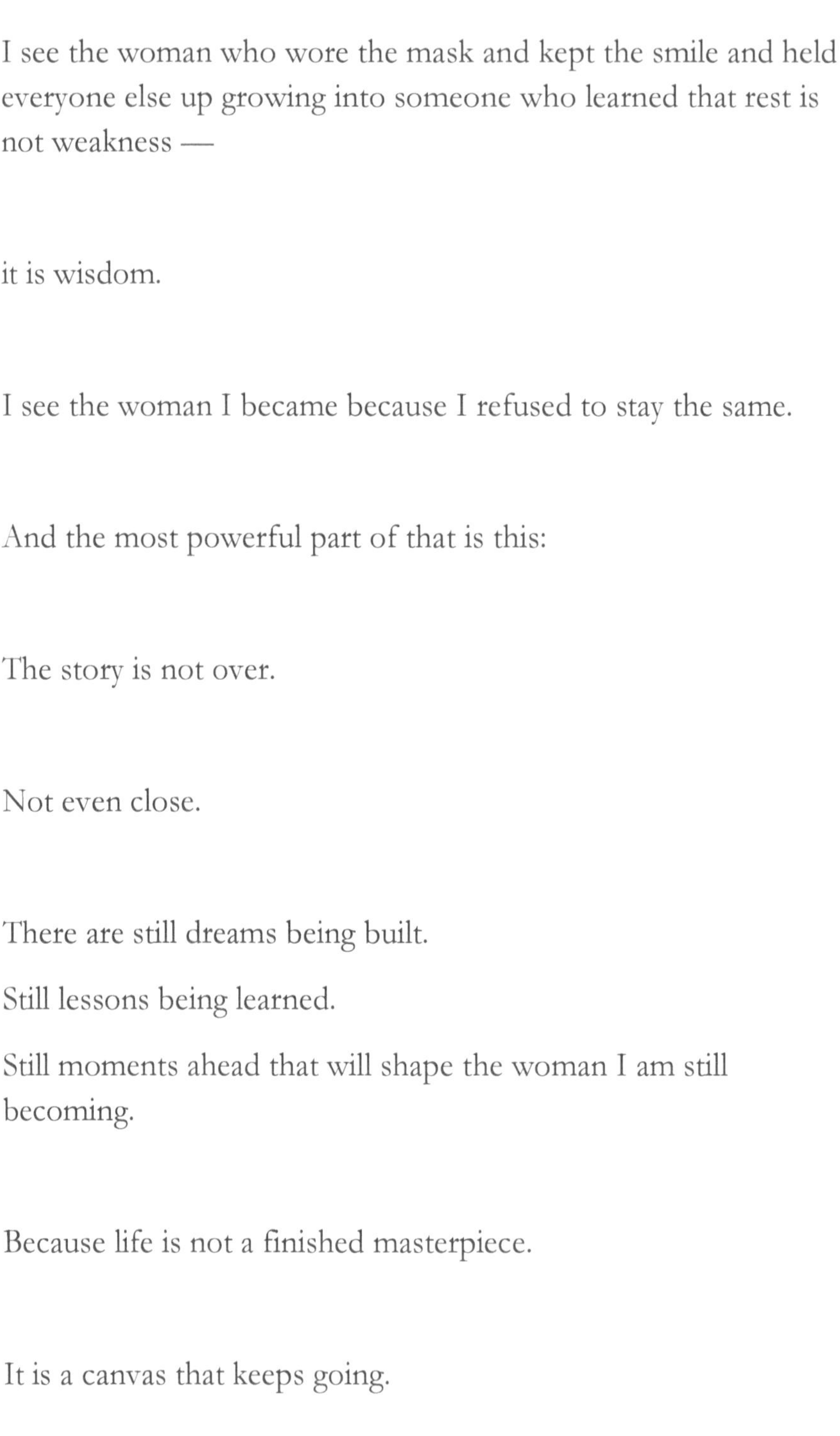

I see the woman who wore the mask and kept the smile and held everyone else up growing into someone who learned that rest is not weakness —

it is wisdom.

I see the woman I became because I refused to stay the same.

And the most powerful part of that is this:

The story is not over.

Not even close.

There are still dreams being built.

Still lessons being learned.

Still moments ahead that will shape the woman I am still becoming.

Because life is not a finished masterpiece.

It is a canvas that keeps going.

And every chapter — even the painful ones, especially the painful ones — adds depth to the picture.

If there is one thing I hope you carry with you after reading this book, it is this:

You do not have to wait until your life is perfect to believe in your future.

You do not have to wait until everything is figured out to begin again.

And you do not have to pretend your life has been easy to recognize the strength it took to make it this far.

Sometimes the greatest victory is simply this:

You survived. You learned. You grew. And you are still standing.

And if you are still standing —

your story is still being written.

This is not my ending.

It is a threshold.

The journey continues. The lessons keep coming. The blessings keep arriving in forms I did not predict. And who knows what the next chapter holds — the next venture, the next love, the next version of this life that surprises me.

I am the author. I still have the pen.

And so do you.

Before you close this book:

Write down three things you are still believing for. Not wishes — declarations. Speak them out loud. Put them somewhere you will see them.

Then take one step toward one of them today.

Not when things settle. Not when it feels right.

Today.

Because the life you are building does not start when everything lines up.

It starts when you decide you are worth building it for.

Romans 8:28 — "And we know that in all things God works for the good of those who love him, who have been called according to his purpose."

What this means to me: All things. Not the easy ones. Not the ones that made sense in the moment. All of it — the losses, the setbacks, the seasons I would not have chosen — working together toward something good. I have seen that prove itself in my own life enough times to build everything on it.

"Starting over is not failure. It is wisdom with experience. She is wiser now. Sharper. Still building. Still believing. Still standing — and she is just getting started."

— *Coach Candace TW*

"I am not who I used to be, and I'm not who I'm going to be yet — but I'm standing in the middle of becoming, and that is more powerful than I ever imagined."

— *Coach Candace TW*

# A Final Word —

# To Everyone Who Made It Here

If you made it here, thank you.

Not just for reading the words. For walking through the journey with me. For sitting in the hard chapters and not looking away. For trusting me with your time and the private corners of your heart where you let these pages land.

Some of what I shared was not easy to say out loud. Some of these lessons took years to understand. Some of these stories still carry pieces of my heart inside them. And some of them — the ones I held the longest, the ones I almost did not write — those are the ones I believe somebody needed the most.

So, if even one part of this book made you pause. If even one sentence reminded you that you are not alone in what you are carrying. If even one moment helped you believe again when life felt too heavy to hold —

Then every word was worth writing.

Before I close these pages, I want to say something to my mother.

I hesitated more than once about what to share in this book. Not because the story was not mine to tell — but because I love her. I did not want anyone to read these pages and see her as anything less than the woman she is. She gave me her blessing. She said: it is your story, tell it. And that meant everything to me.

Mom — you are loved. You are respected. You are appreciated. And you have been forgiven in the fullest sense of that word. I do not want you to carry what you have been carrying. Put it down. We are here now. And now is good.

You are not behind.

You are not too late.

You are not too much.

And you are not too far gone.

Whatever chapter you are standing in right now — whether it feels like clarity or chaos — it is not your final chapter.

You are still in the middle of becoming.

I also want to say something directly to the people whose stories are woven into mine.

I did not write this book to wound anyone. I wrote it because healing required me to tell the truth. And telling the truth required a courage I had to build over years. If you read something in these pages that sat heavy with you, I hope you also read the grace underneath it. Because it was always there. Even in the hardest parts. Especially in the hardest parts.

To my children — Ronnie, Laniyah, and Mann.

You are my greatest chapters. The ones I would write again even knowing everything they would cost me. I hope when you read this book you see a mother who was not perfect, but who loved you with everything she had. I hope you see yourselves the way I see you — as people who are still becoming something extraordinary. I hope you carry the lessons, release the weight, and write your own stories with the kind of honesty and courage it takes to truly live.

I am so proud of you. All three of you. Always.

Now I want to say something to the person reading this who thinks their time has passed.

The one who looks at where they are and wonders if they are too far behind. Too old. Too broken. Too late to start again.

You are not.

There is a true story — later portrayed in a film — about a man named Chris Gardner. He was broke, homeless, raising his young son, sleeping in shelters and subway bathrooms while fighting his way through an unpaid internship with nothing but determination and the refusal to accept that his beginning would determine his end. What he came from should have stopped him. What he went through would have broken most people. But he kept going. And what he built on the other side of that season became something the world needed to witness.

His beginning did not determine his end.

And neither does yours.

I have watched people go back to school after their children graduated and walk across that stage right alongside them. I have seen people build something meaningful at fifty, sixty, seventy — because they finally stopped waiting for permission and decided to begin. I have read about people who had nothing, who started over from the floor, who became something that made the world stop and pay attention. Not because the timing was perfect. Because they refused to quit while they still had breath.

As long as you are breathing, you have time.

Not to rewrite what already happened — you cannot do that. But to keep writing what comes next. To add chapters that surprise you. To become, in this next season, the fullest version of who you were always meant to be.

Your story does not stop at the age someone told you it should. It does not stop at the setback that tried to define you. It does not stop because someone looked at where you are and decided you should be further along by now.

It stops when you put down the pen.

And you are not done writing.

Because the truth is — life really does be life'n.

Plans change. People disappoint. Dreams take longer than expected. Roads take turns that were never on the map. You look up sometimes and barely recognize the chapter you are standing in.

But through every season I have lived — the good ones, the painful ones, the confusing ones, the ones I would not wish on anyone — one truth has never changed:

God still God'n.

Even in the chaos. Even in the waiting. Even in the seasons where nothing was clear and the prayers felt like they were going nowhere and I was holding faith with both hands just to keep it from slipping.

Grace was there.

I could not always see it in the moment. But looking back, I can trace it through everything. The door that opened just in time. The person who showed up exactly when they were needed. The prayer answered in a form I did not recognize until later. The table that turned when I had stopped watching for it to turn.

He was carrying me. Even when I thought I was carrying myself.

And if grace carried me through the chapters you just read — I believe with everything in me that it will carry you through yours too.

This is not my ending.

It is a threshold. The journey continues. The lessons keep coming. The blessings keep arriving in forms I did not predict. I am still becoming. Still building. Still believing for things that have not yet shown up in the forms I imagined. And I do not know what the next chapter holds — the next venture, the next love, the next version of this life that surprises me. But I am walking toward it with more wisdom, more faith, and more of myself than I have ever had before.

I am the author. I still have the pen.

And so do you.

Before you leave this moment — pause.

Take a breath.

And acknowledge how far you have come.

Not how far you have to go.

How far you have come.

Because that version of you — the one who kept going — deserves to be recognized.

So wherever life finds you right now — whatever chapter you are standing in, whatever you are still waiting for, whatever you are still healing from or building toward —

Keep going.

Keep writing.

Keep believing that what is coming is worth staying for.

Your story is not finished.

And neither is mine.

With every ounce of love I have —

—Candace Travis

Coach Candace TW

I Am A Transforming Woman

Grace in the middle of chaos.

Always.

*Some stories don't end when the chapter closes.*

*Some stories rise.*

*This is what rising sounds like.*

## *Grace In the Middle of Chaos*

They handed me silence like it was a gift.
Like if I folded myself small enough…
tucked my truth between my ribs…
pressed my voice so far down it forgot what air felt like —
maybe… just maybe…
the pain would be polite enough to leave.
It wasn't.

Pain don't knock.
Pain moves in.
Rearranges your furniture.
Sleeps in your bed.
Answers your door.
Smiles at your company —
while you sit there pretending everything is fine.
And I got good at fine.
…
Lord — I got real good at fine.

But God still God'n.
Even when life was life'n —
grace showed up in the middle of the chaos.
Every. Single. Time.

I was fifteen…
carrying more than a baby —
carrying a story I didn't have language for yet.
I was a woman pouring rivers into people…
who handed me back empty cups…
and called it love.
I was the light in every room —

while something inside me was still looking for a window.
Smile on. Mask up. Show out.
Because strong women?
…
We don't fall apart in public.
We fall apart in the car.
In the shower.
At 2AM —
when the house is quiet…
and the only witness left…
is God.
And He saw me.
Every. Single. Time.

But God still God'n.
Even when life was life'n —
grace showed up in the middle of the chaos.
Every. Single. Time.

The jar got heavy.
Carrying what was done to me like it was mine to own.
Wearing shame like a hand-me-down coat —
didn't fit… never did…
but I wore it anyway —
because somebody put it on my shoulders
before I knew I could take it off.
And the body?
…
The body keeps score.
Mine had been tallying for years.
Dis-ease in the spirit… becomes disease in the body.
And I know that —
not from a textbook —
but from a hospital bed…

from anxiety attacks…
in the middle of a life that looked fine…
from the outside.
Fine.
…
I was so tired of fine.

But God still God'n.
Even when life was life'n —
grace showed up in the middle of the chaos.
Every. Single. Time.

Then something shifted.
Not loud. Not dramatic.
Not movie-script perfect with background music and timing.
It was quiet.
Like a seed… deciding… it was done waiting.
I forgave.
Not because it didn't hurt —
but because I deserved peace.
I kept the lessons. I dropped the weight.
I forgave the woman in the mirror —
who stayed too long…
in places that were never built to hold her.
And I said —
baby…
you were never the problem.
And this time?
…
I believed it.

Tables turn.
Prayers work.
What was planted in the dark — always finds the light.

I started speaking life over things that looked like graves.
Started planting seeds in soil that didn't clap for me.
Started showing up when nobody was watching —
because I finally understood —
the harvest doesn't need an audience.
It just needs a woman who won't quit.
I kept posting when four people were watching.
I kept building when the doors closed.
I kept praying when it felt like I was talking to the ceiling —
until the ceiling opened.
Until the room filled.
Until a woman walked up to me and said —
"Because of you… I didn't quit."
And I stood there…
receiving…
what I had been planting into silence for years.

Tables turn.
Prayers work.
What was planted in the dark — always finds the light.

So let me tell you what healing really sounds like.
It doesn't sound like perfection.
It sounds like a woman who stopped apologizing for surviving.
It sounds like laughter in a room full of grief —
because even in loss… we chose to remember the joy.
It sounds like — "This too shall pass" —
whispered on a cold morning…
right before grace knocks on your door…
with an answer you forgot you prayed for.
That's not coincidence.
That's confirmation.

Life be life'n.
But God still God'n.
And I am still —
still —
STILL —
standing.

I picked up the pen.
After twenty years of silence —
after the weight… after the drowning…
after surviving in plain sight —
I picked it up.
Not because everything is perfect.
Not because the story is finished.
Not because I finally became who I thought I had to be to speak.
I picked it up…
because the truth was always mine.
Because some stories —
don't ask permission.
They rise.

Like breath after being held too long.
Like a woman who finally remembers —
she was never meant to shrink to survive.

So if life has been life'n on you — keep going.
If the jar got heavy — put it down.
If they took your voice and tried to make it shame — pick it back up.
Because the place that tried to bury you…
…
didn't know it was planting you.

And everything you survived —
every tear… every valley… every silent battle —
was building a woman the world has been waiting for.
She is wiser now.
Softer where she needed softening.
Stronger where she needed steel.
Still building.
Still becoming.
Still standing —
on everything that tried to break her.
She picked up the pen.
And this time —
…
she's not putting it down.

Life be life'n.
But God still God'n.
And I —
…
I am still here.

***Grace showed up in the middle of the chaos.***

***Life be life'n…but God still God'n.***

# Stay Connected

If this book spoke to you…

If something in these pages met you exactly where you are…

I would love to hear from you.

Share your experience.

Share the moment that stayed with you.

Share what shifted.

You can connect with me or follow the journey here:

Instagram: @transformwithcandacetw

Facebook: Transforming Woman / Candace TW

TikTok: @transformwithcandacetw

If you share this book, use:

#GraceInTheMiddleOfChaos

So, I can see it, support you, and celebrate your journey with you.

This is bigger than a book.

This is healing.

This is growth.

This is becoming.

And now…You're part of it.

# About the Author

Candace Travis is a certified fitness coach, motivational speaker, and the founder of Transforming Woman — a platform rooted in the belief that true transformation begins in the mind before it ever shows up in the body.

Known to her community as Coach Candace TW, she has spent years pouring into people across Chicago and beyond — in gyms, in challenges, in living rooms, and across digital platforms — helping them rebuild not just their physical health, but their mental, emotional, and spiritual well-being.

But her work is not just about bodies — it is about becoming.

A mother of three, a conqueror, and a woman of deep faith, Candace knows firsthand what it means to start over — more than once. She has rebuilt businesses from the ground up, navigated the end of a marriage, walked through grief, battled anxiety, and found her way back to purpose through prayer, therapy, and the decision to keep going when quitting would have been easier.

Grace in the Middle of Chaos is her debut book — and her most honest offering yet.

It is the story she was not sure she was brave enough to tell.

And the one somebody needed to hear.

"The comeback is always louder than the setback — if you don't quit on yourself."

— Coach Candace TW

www.ingramcontent.com/pod-product-compliance
Ingram Content Group UK Ltd.
Pitfield, Milton Keynes, MK11 3LW, UK
UKHW041857190726
13854UKWH00002B/948